UNDERSTANDING POVERTY IN AFRICA?
A Navigation through Disputed Concepts, Data and Terrains

Mats Hårsmar

NORDISKA AFRIKAINSTITUTET, UPPSALA 2010

INDEXING TERMS:
Economic conditions
Poverty
Agricultural development
Poverty alleviation
Development research
Development theory
Case studies
Burkina Faso
Tanzania
Africa south of Sahara

Language checking: Peter Colenbrander
ISSN 0280-2171
ISBN 978-91-7106-668-8
© the author and Nordiska Afrikainstitutet 2010
Grafisk form Elin Olsson, ELBA Grafisk Produktion

CONTENTS

FOREWORD

The eradication of poverty and, by extension, the achievement of universal well-being has always been central to the language and practice of development. However, the development record of the past 50 years has been mixed. Although some progress has been made in human well-being in most countries, literally billions of people remain in a state of dire deprivation and hopelessness. This is particularly true of sub-Saharan Africa.

Despite the slow progress in eradicating poverty, our approach to understanding poverty has grown in recent years. There is increasing recognition that poverty is a complex, multidimensional phenomenon that spans both material and non-material aspects of life. Thus, an understanding of poverty and deprivation in Africa requires an analytical framework that encompasses various dimensions. These include the need to

- link poverty with employment and social integration;
- link the economic and the political and social dimensions of poverty;
- understand the role of social processes and institutional structures in creating deprivation or generating inclusion;
- understand the impact of globalisation on anti-poverty strategies; and
- explore social and economic rights and access to employment, livelihoods and markets.

This discussion paper by Dr. Mats Harsmar is the first in a series to be published by the Research Cluster on Globalization, Trade and Regional Integration under the rubric "Poverty, Inequality and Social Exclusion in Africa." With three-year funding from SIDA, the programme seeks to build a cohesive network of partnerships with key research centres, civil society groups and think tanks in Africa and Europe to generate innovate research, catalyse public debate and to inform public policy so as to make economic globalisation pro-poor and more inclusive of Africa. We hope readers will find this first report informative and we invite interested friends of Africa to join in the debate and to be part of the solution.

Professor Fantu Cheru
Research Director and Coordinator of the Research Cluster on Globalization,
Trade and Regional Integration
The Nordic Africa Institute

INTRODUCTION

Pervasive poverty implies distorted development and malfunctioning societies. Hence, in social science in general and development studies in particular the study of poverty remains central, particularly in studies of African societies. Beyond the obvious fact that sub-Saharan Africa is the region with the most pervasive poverty levels in any international comparison, a social science research focus in this part of the world implies studies of numerous dynamics, processes and situations that link to poverty issues. The sheer prevalence of poverty makes it an important factor in describing and understanding African societies.

No matter how we approach the study of poverty, the task is of critical importance. In order to deal with one of the major global challenges of our time, there is a need for a deeper understanding, particularly if we wish to become more practical in dealing with poverty. What are the paths that seem most promising in achieving this deeper understanding of poverty with a focus on sub-Saharan Africa? To answer this question, work is needed at the theoretical and methodological as well as empirical levels.

This volume contains two separate articles. The first provides an overview of major conceptual positions on poverty and focuses on theoretical and methodological issues relating to the debate on how to understand what poverty is and how it can be measured. The article agrees with the view that the epistemological and normative aspects have not been emphasised sufficiently in the discussions on the need for increased multidisciplinary work on poverty. These aspects form the fundamental dividing lines in the poverty debate. However, the article goes on to argue that the fairly recent emergence of the capability approach to the study of poverty provides a possible and promising platform for bridging most of these divides.

The second article is an empirical study of recent poverty developments in Tanzania and Burkina Faso. Common to both these countries – one in East and the other in West Africa – is that a largely subsistent agricultural sector dominates their economies. The article builds on a combination of quantitative and qualitative methods and describes the importance of regional differences in agricultural development for the evolution of poverty in these countries.

ACCNOWLEDGEMENTS

This work has greatly benefitted from comments on earlier versions by colleagues at the Nordic Africa Institute, and Knut Christian Myhre in particular. Substantive comments were also received from John Hammock, and in particular from Howard Stein, who took time to read and comment on the whole manuscript in a most constructive way. Michel Koné and Yembi Olivier Souli at the INSD in Burkina Faso helped out with statistics, Peter Colenbrander provided language checking, Sonja Johansson and Birgitta Hellmark-Lindgren took care of the editing work. Many thanks to all of you. Final responsibility for the weaknesses of the text remains with the author.

1. CONCEPTS OF POVERTY

1.1 Introduction – Poverty is multidimensional

Even though approaches to the study of poverty and poverty dynamics are manifold, there is an emerging consensus on the need for a multidimensional understanding of poverty (Addison, Hulme and Kanbur 2008). Many attempts are being made at furthering methods and concepts in this direction. In applying the differing measures, the empirical result has often been only partial overlap between different measurements. This suggests that multidimensional measures provide richer descriptions of poverty, and who the poor are, than measures such as one dollar a day (Alkire and Foster 2008). However, no firm conclusions and no consensus have been reached on the best way to proceed towards multidimensionality.[1]

As well, based on an extended dialogue between an economist and an anthropologist on issues related to methodologies and underlying perspectives, Kanbur and Shaffer (2005) have arrived at further proposals for improved studies of poverty. Their basic message is that poverty analyses need to become increasingly dynamic, multidimensional and cross-disciplinary. They call for more combined quantitative and qualitative methods. However, they argue that even with such approaches tensions based on philosophical grounds will remain. In particular, they identify tensions regarding epistemology and normative theory as the most pervasive. At the same time, there exist counter-positions that argue more on the level of principle that the kind of epistemological differences that are at play here are possible to overcome.

Kanbur and Shaffer (2005) and Shaffer (1996) have made rather thorough analyses of the philosophical and methodological differences between various poverty concepts. We will refer to these in a description of some influential approaches to the study of poverty. We will also discuss Kanbur and Shaffer's argument. Do the difficulties in finding a coherent and common approach to the study of poverty rest on epistemological, methodological or possibly ideological grounds? Or is it a combination of these? What are the possibilities for overcoming such differences? A particular point we discuss is whether the move towards multidisciplinarity and multidimensional concepts of poverty imply progress towards a more widely shared concept of poverty.

1.2 Theoretical framework

In describing and discussing the analysis by Kanbur and Shaffer (2005), we need a theoretical framework. The basic elements of this are the different epistemological positions. Epistemology deals with the question of knowledge: what can we know, and how do we know what we know? The epistemological differences Kanbur and Shaffer refer to can in their purified form be captured as a distinction between the concepts of explaining and interpreting. Ultimately, we may trace these two positions back to Aristotle and Galileo respectively. Where the former dealt with issues of motivation and action, the latter focused on cause and effect. Throughout the history of science, the tension between positions focusing on understanding and those focusing on explanation has been dominant (von Wright 1971). These positions can be classified as naturalistic or empirical and hermeneutic (interpretive).

The naturalistic position – with its roots going back to Galileo – builds on research methods developed by the natural sciences but later adapted to social sciences. It searches

---

1. Refer, for instance, to the ongoing debates at www.QSquared.ca, Wider and at OPHI, among others.

for causal laws through the gathering of data by observation and experiment. Historically, an important influence for such positions is the British empiricist tradition, associated with names such as John Locke, George Berkeley and David Hume. For instance, Locke argued in a debate with the rationalist Rene Descartes that the only knowledge people may have is *a posteriori* knowledge – that is what they know based on their experiences (Locke 1689). In the naturalist tradition, the unit of knowledge is "sense-datum". This refers to a unit that has no "… element in it of reading, or interpretation, which is a brute datum" (Taylor 1985:19). Objective evidence is those observations of phenomena that are independent of feelings or thoughts (Rosenberg 1988:110).

Hermeneutics, on the other hand, deals with the interpretation of social meaning, and may be traced all the way back to Aristotle. Originally a method for the analysis of texts, in particular biblical texts, the approach was broadened during the early 19th century by people such as Schleiermacher and later Dilthey to all forms of communication and social phenomena. With this broadening, hermeneutics lost its traditional relationship to sacred texts as conveyors of truth. However, in modern hermeneutics, the concept of truth has been regained. Since the human being is in the world, it is possible for her through a historic process of understanding to present and correct and reveal truth (Lübcke 1988:227). But hermeneutics does not necessarily apply the same notion of truth as the naturalistic position, with its view of truth as correspondence to reality (Shaffer 1996:28). Contrary to the naturalistic position, hermeneutics further claims that scientific inquiry is always interpretive. Social sciences must even deal with a "double hermeneutics", where scientific and research paradigms must be interpreted at the theoretical level, and conceptual schemes and meaning structures must be interpreted at the level of data collection (Giddens 1976:158, 162).

There are others who argue that the tensions between Aristotle and Galileo can in principle be overcome. The basis for this is a third epistemological position. In his book *Slaget om Verkligheten* (The Battle over Reality), Kristensson Uggla (2002) discusses the interrelationship between interpretation and explanation. In doing so, he emphasises the importance of interpretation and the role that hermeneutics must play if we are to relate our actions and reflections to the constantly changing societies we live in. Explanations may be necessary, but may prove less meaningful if they deal with irrelevant phenomena. On the other hand, hermeneutics must avoid falling into relativism and provide *improved* understanding in relation to what explanations may provide. To achieve this, hermeneutics must itself include processes of explanation. Kristensson Uggla seeks his response to this challenge in the concept of *critical interpretation*, which has been developed by Paul Ricoeur and others (ibid., p. 338f). Instead of separating explanation and understanding, these concepts are combined in a process of interpretation in which explanation conveys or transmits understanding.

Even Shaffer describes and analyses the position of critical interpretation or critical hermeneutics as developed by Jürgen Habermas (Shaffer 1996). In this he also refers to Habermas's consensual theory of truth, where the potential agreement of all others is the fundamental condition. According to this position, validity is based on truth, rightness, comprehensibility and sincerity, where the first two must be justified by rational argumentation leading to consensus (Habermas 1979). The criterion for true consensus is procedural: it depends on a process of open dialogue, the "Ideal Speech Situation (ISS)", to which all concerned have access; in which participants recognise each other as autonomous agents; where there is equal opportunity for dialogue; and where there is freedom to question traditional norms. ISS is a constitutive condition for rational speech, as well as a guide for social action: it provides the basis for a critique of both facts and values, and thus provides a basis for truthful normative positions.

However, despite his use and acceptance of critical hermeneutics, Shaffer (1996) and later Kanbur and Shaffer (2005) not only conclude that there are important epistemological differences between various conceptualisations of poverty, but also that these differences will remain. This will be further discussed below. In addressing the various approaches to poverty, we try to establish whether these fundamental tensions can be overcome or not.

1.3 How has the poverty debate evolved?

The scientific discipline most influential in setting the poverty agenda has been development economics. In this tradition, the focus has most often been on measuring levels of poverty. Hence, research has largely been driven by a functional objective, by a search for policy relevance at an instrumental level. In order to measure poverty levels, descriptions of poverty have been a necessary complement. A materially oriented "head-count" approach to poverty has been given centrality and static descriptions of poverty levels have been the default position. Increasingly, however, there has been a move towards dynamic perspectives. This move has been driven by the development of methods within econometrics and the availability of improved data. In particular, increased use of panel data and improved modelling have played a role. However, the shift has also been driven by continuing conceptual work.[2]

In the field of poverty studies, both theoretical and methodological starting points are required. Various approaches have emerged combining theoretical and methodological perspectives. However, in the interests of clarity these starting points are discussed separately. Hence, we start with a description of how poverty concepts have been driven by diverging theoretical perspectives. The criteria we have used for the selection of the definitions of poverty we describe is that they have resulted in a substantial amount of academic work; they have been used in applied analysis of poverty; and they have relevance for a more general public discussion of poverty.

Income and consumption as a base

Historically, the first definition of poverty to emerge was the *subsistence approach*, which arose in 19th century Victorian England. This was a perspective developed by nutritionists and centred on physiological or material needs. According to this approach, poverty was defined as "the minimum necessaries for maintaining merely physical efficiency". This included clothing, fuel, housing and, first and foremost, food. The approach saw human needs as mainly physical, but not social, and has great similarities with what nowadays is labelled *material approaches* to poverty. One extended version of the latter is the *monetary approach*, in which indicators for the measurement of poverty have been both income and consumption levels, although there may be variation in what assets are included in material or monetary poverty definitions. However, a common thread is that all these approaches are based on utility theory (Townsend 2006; Chambers 2006).

On the surface, measuring poverty in money metrics might seem straightforward, and comparability seems assured especially where the same currency is used across countries. This is the logic behind the $US 1/day measure, which is widely used and applied as an

---

2. Addison et al. 2008. For a historical perspective on the poverty concept, see, for instance, Ehrenpreis 2009.

international standard by the World Bank. However, there are complications. The currently used level, US$ 1.25 /day, is calculated on the basis of the mean of national poverty lines in the poor countries. This implies that whenever a new calculation is made, comparability with previous poverty lines is lost. More specifically, the current "dollar-a-day" line corresponds to the value of goods and services that US$ 1.25 could buy in the US in 2005 prices. The value of these goods is then calculated for each and every country (purchasing power parity). The previously used poverty line was calculated as the value that US$ 1.08 could buy in the US in 1993 prices, which corresponded to the mean of poor countries poverty lines in that year (Ravallion et al. 2008:16).

If one were to compare these two poverty lines, inflation in the US would have to be taken into consideration. A 1993 poverty line, corrected for US inflation, would have meant a 2005 poverty line of US$ 1.45/day, which is substantially higher than the current one. This means that a comparison between the 1993 and the 2005 poverty lines would underestimate the current number of poor people in the world. It turns out that even a previous adjustment of the dollar-a-day poverty line (from US$ 1/day in 1985 prices) went in the same direction. An inflation-corrected poverty line from 1985 would have meant a poverty line of US$ 1.81/day in 2005. These different poverty lines are not meant to be compared (ibid.). However, the popularity and seeming simplicity of the lines make such comparisons almost unavoidable. The consequence is that reductions in global poverty become seriously overestimated.

In addition to problems related to fluctuating exchange rates and inflation levels, the issue of what goods to base the purchasing power calculation on also complicates the measuring. Should basic goods consumed by the total population, or goods primarily consumed by the poor, be included? And what if poor people consume different goods in different countries? The US$ 1/day measure includes all goods and services in relation to how much they are consumed on average internationally. Prices of basic necessities play a minor role in this measure, while they are of great importance to poor people (Robeyns 2005:31ff).

In the context of material approaches to poverty, mention should also be made of a more recent phenomenon, *pro-poor economic growth*. This emerged in the 1990s, based on the finding that the impact of economic growth on poverty reduction differed between various societies – the *poverty elasticity* differed. Obviously, this approach starts from the assumption that economic growth leads to poverty reduction. The question is how to make economic growth benefit the poor as much as possible.

There is also a debate about how to define pro-poor growth. The *absolute* definition looks solely at the effect of economic growth on the poor. When economic growth leads to increasing incomes among the poor, then growth is said to be pro-poor. By contrast, the *relative* definition claims that growth is only pro-poor if growth benefits poor people and inequalities simultaneously decrease. The absolute definition is more commonly used, supported by the argument that the poor would benefit more in terms of income if overall economic growth is faster, even though it is not reducing inequality. In situations of economic growth, inequality may be kept stable or increase (that is, this position is open to the "trickle down" theory). To measure pro-poor growth, the Rate of Pro Poor Growth (RPPG) is used. This refers to the mean growth rate of consumption by households situated below a certain poverty line, which is defined in terms of income. However, the underlying assumption that economic growth leads to poverty reduction may be questioned on empirical grounds. One study undertaken by the UNDP International Poverty Centre, looked at cases of economic growth in 80 countries during the period 1984-2001. In total, 237 spells of growth were studied. Only 55 of these – some 23 percent – were found to have been pro-poor. The others either did not result in per capita consumption growth (economic growth lower than population growth – 45 percent) or were outright cases of anti-poor growth (32 percent) (Son and Kakwani 2006).

Material approaches to poverty such as the above, focusing exclusively on individuals, have not gone unchallenged. An initial rather mild critique came in the 1970s when the *basic needs approach* was developed by the International Labour Organization, ILO. It was similar to the subsistence approach in that it built on what was perceived as minimum needs for a family. However, the basic needs approach extended this group of needs to include essential services that were provided not only by the market, but also by and for the community at large, such as safe water, sanitation, public transport, healthcare, education and cultural activities. The needs were also extended from what is required by an individual to include those things required by local communities and populations more widely through the inclusion of public goods. "Needs" were seen as different from "wants", and the concept of basic needs was used to prioritise among wants. Not all wants are of equal importance. Some goods are necessary in order for people to reproduce, to function in and contribute to their societies. In other words, the basic needs discourse rejected the market as the sole and optimal provider of goods and services (Gasper 1996:3). Obviously, this approach carried within itself a strong critique of economic policies that prioritised pure market-based solutions. In this way, the academic debate revealed that there was also a political aspect of the debate on how to define poverty.

A debate followed about the distinction between felt needs and justified needs. The basis for this debate was the difficulty in distinguishing between the positive (factual) use of the term and the normative (ibid., p. 5), but also the lack of clarity on the basis to be used in determining which needs are more fundamental than others. In other words, it was not really clear what the term "basic" in basic needs should refer to. Three distinct starting points were discernable: i) *Positive* theories that explain behaviour as driven by "needs". Abraham Maslow´s hierarchy of needs is perhaps the most famous theory in this category; ii) Theories that identify prerequisites for various levels and types of functioning, such as physical and mental health. These theories try to explain what makes people happy or content, and they focus on the *instrumental* needs for fulfilling such ends; iii) Theories that are based on *normative* statements that prioritise some prerequisites, and thus are ethical theories of needs (ibid., p. 9f).

All the above positions – from the subsistence approach to the basic needs approach – may be classified as belonging to an income/consumption (I/C) approach to poverty. What it means to be poor, the ill-being, is defined externally by a third party as a deprivation of physical needs due to insufficient private consumption. The measurement is quantitative and addresses either income or consumption, and is usually based on questionnaire surveys. The consumer has free choice and is assumed to allocate resources in ways that maximise the fulfilment of basic needs. All these positions more or less belong to the naturalistic or empiricist tradition described above. What they also have in common is that the normative theory underpinning them is utilitarianism. There are direct historical links between the naturalist normative theory/utilitarianism and the I/C position (Kanbur and Shaffer 2005).

In its original version, utilitarianism stresses that utility or "happiness" should be maximised across individuals, and that this social outcome is the benchmark against which social states should be evaluated. Bentham called this the "greatest happiness principle" (Bentham 1789). Despite Bentham's claim that pleasure and pain are directly measurable, the problem of measuring utility or happiness in an interpersonal way led to a shift towards the revealed preferences approach. In the latter, the maximal satisfaction of preferences – revealed by consumer choice – is the ultimate benchmark. It was further claimed that this is measurable through a money metric (Samuelson 1966; Kanbur and Shaffer 2005:16).

Social relations and poverty

There are as well a number of poverty concepts that are determined more on the basis of social relations than on pure consumption. The discussion above about how to define what a justifiable basic need is already opened the way for this. It was during the 1990s that another major approach emerged stressing that poverty is based on *relative deprivation*. According to this perspective, both material and social conditions matter to poverty. Poor people are those that are denied resources to fulfil social demands and observe the customs and laws of society. Hence, deprivations may take multiple forms, and are fundamentally described in relation to what is seen as normal or a median in society. What are regarded as necessities are, in every society, to some extent defined by custom. A starting point for this approach has been the acknowledgement that even in the subsistence approach some aspects were in fact defined by custom (e.g., the need for a white shirt for Sunday Mass). However, the emphasis on seeing poverty as a relative phenomenon leads to the need to differentiate between inequalities and poverty. In this way, politics and power are introduced into the understanding of poverty.

Variations on this theme put emphasis either on *social exclusion* as the active component in the production of poverty, or stress the deprivation of various capabilities as the source of poverty. The *capability approach* more clearly than other perspectives shifts the emphasis away from resources and means towards ends that people have reason to pursue – and correspondingly, to the freedom they have to reach these ends. It is the deprivation of capabilities, rather than the deprivation of assets or resources, that constitutes poverty. It follows that the opposite of poverty is the freedom to satisfy the valued ends, according to Amartya Sen, who during the 1990s became the best-known proponent of this position (Sen 1999).[3]

Sen makes the distinction between a person's actual achievements, and her or his freedom to achieve. The former represents the combination of established functionings, whereas the latter represents the combination of functionings from which he or she can choose. With poverty viewed as capability deprivation, focus should be on capabilities with intrinsic value, rather than on, for instance, income deprivation, which is of instrumental value. Income is one among a number of factors that negatively influence capabilities. Furthermore, the extent to which income affects capabilities varies between different communities, families and individuals. This is an important reason capability deprivation must be seen in more than income terms. With this shift from material resources to capabilities, social relations are fully brought into the understanding of poverty, while the possibility of observing distinct aspects of poverty is retained. The capability approach still allows for measuring poverty, but moves away from its narrow material definition.

---

3. The approach was developed in dialogue with Martha C. Nussbaum.

Still another shift places the emphasis on the agents, rather than the observers, as the ones establishing what poverty is and how it should be interpreted. The multiplicity of meanings of poverty stems from the *participative approach,* which claims that ultimately only poor people themselves can establish the meaning of poverty and assess who the poor are. While this position implies that possibilities of comparing different communities are lost, what is gained is a deeper understanding of the subjectivity of poverty and they way people define and look upon themselves (Chambers 2006). One major advantage of participatory approaches is that they are able to deal with situations where commonly used concepts of poverty do not correspond with local people's perceptions of who is poor. For instance, among pastoralist groups in East Africa, "the poor" are seen as not belonging to their society, since those who own cattle are perceived as not being poor. Persons who happen to be deprived of their cattle are placed in the category of the poor, but they are simultaneously excluded from the pastoralist society. The poor are in this way defined away as pastoralists, since pastoralists don't allow themselves to be regarded as poor. This practice becomes increasingly problematic when the pastoralists are facing growing problems of feeding themselves or earning monetary income, despite the fact that they still control cattle (Anderson and Broch-Due 1999). Descriptions of pastoralist societies also indicate that material approaches to poverty may be misleading, since pastoralists migrating to urban areas are suddenly much more dependent on material goods and monetary income than they were in rural areas in order to fulfil identical basic human functions. Food, clothing, shelter and a long list of other things suddenly cost money. This makes comparisons between people from the same society, but living in different localities, impossible if monetary measures are used (Lesamana 2009:68f).

Furthermore, members of certain societies do use goods to build social relations rather than for consumption. For instance, poor people may provide gifts to rich people who have fallen ill, rather than consume extremely scarce resources themselves: they invest in social relations (Berry 1985, 1993). In such a case, the object (the poor person) personifies him- or herself through redistribution. This is quite distinct from situations where producers objectify themselves through production, and social relationships are used to produce things. When the focus is – as in the former situation – on the distribution and exchange of things, the aim is to establish and maintain social relationships. Mention is sometimes made of being "rich in people". In such situations, disposability, rather than possession or property, is central. What people strive for in such situations is not primarily their own consumption – even if they live in what might sometimes be described as poverty – but social relationships. Whether or not these relationships are nurtured with the long-term objective of maximizing or smoothing consumption over time is less relevant for the immediate study of poverty. In situations such as these, it would still be more relevant to measure access to relations rather than access to consumption goods, since this would come closer to how people themselves define poverty and who the poor are.

Above, we have grouped a number of positions together under the I/C approach to poverty. Would it be relevant to also group those positions together that have some kind of social relationship as a common thread? If so, how would such a group be labelled? Shaffer (1996) makes his analytical distinction precisely between the I/C approach and what he calls the Participatory Approach (PA). It is the differences between these two stylised positions that he discusses in terms of epistemology and normative theory.

In PA, the definition of who is poor builds on an interactive process, a participatory poverty assessment (PPA), which involves both internal and external actors, namely the population in question and the researcher. The data used may be both quantitative (most often of ordinal character, rather than cardinal) and qualitative. They are generated in a communicative or discursive way, and include local conceptual categories. The consumer preferences are not taken at face value, as they are in the I/C approach, but are criticised both by participants and outside observers in a dialogue. Poverty concepts within PA tend to be broader than in the I/C position, and include "physical, social, political, psychological/spiritual elements" (Chambers 1995:vi). PA belongs to the hermeneutic philosophical tradition described above, with interpretation as its central element. The normative theory underpinning PA is discursive normative theory or discourse ethics. This is a procedural theory, since the central element is that normative conclusions can only be reached if an actual dialogue takes place. There are a number of conditions regarding the forms of this process relating to the character of speech. First, for any norm to be valid "… all affected can accept the consequences and side effects its general observance can be anticipated to have for the satisfaction of everyone's interests" (Habermas 1991:65). If this is to be the case, the ISS described above is a necessary condition.

We will apply Shaffer's categorisation, but with important extensions. Even if it is analytically clear, Shaffer's distinction seems too blunt, since, for instance, the capability approach takes a middle position regarding many of the divergent issues. Hence, we treat Shaffer's two opposing positions as poles on an axis along which intermediate positions are possible.

1.4 Poverty concepts compared

Shaffer identifies fundamental differences in the following parameters of the I/C and the PA positions: i) definition of poverty; ii) measurement of poverty; iii) position on consumer preferences; iv) sources of data; and v) research objectives and sources of poverty. It is in relation to these aspects that various epistemological and normative positions are influential and become explicit. We describe and discuss each of these in the following section.

Differences at the level of epistemology and normative theory also translate into different positions regarding the methodologies that are chosen. Building on numerous attempts at combining methodologies, Kanbur (2003) and Kanbur and Shaffer (2005) describe the following five dimensions of the fundamental differences between qualitative and quantitative methods :

- Type of information on population – non-numerical to numerical
- Type of population coverage – specific to general
- Type of population involvement – active to passive
- Type of inference method – inductive to deductive
- Type of disciplinary framework – broad social science to neo-classical economics

Methodological differences also include those between quantitative and qualitative methods. The treatment of data as variables in quantitative methods opens the way for generalisations and for inter-subjective assessments. However, at the same time, the treatment of cases as variables implies the loss of valuable information. Context and meaning, as well as some variation, get lost in the process of narrowing down cases into variables. The room for interpretation and deeper understanding of processes is much larger when qualitative methods are applied. On the other hand, such richness implies that representativeness is much lower or even lost.

These methodological differences will be woven into the discussion that follows.

The definition of poverty in the I/C position is done by external agents, using "objective" criteria and applying a deductive approach. Poverty is limited to the sphere of material elements that seemingly lend themselves to quantification, and concerns consumption of goods deemed necessary for survival or a minimum level of existence. By contrast, PA applies to a process in which both internal and external actors take active part and in which more inductive methods are used. The population studied of course enjoys an internal position in such dialogues. In a sense, even the social scientist partly takes an internal position in that s/he interprets and mediates local conceptions of meaning. At the same time, s/he plays an external role by participating only over a limited timespan by bringing in outside knowledge and critical perspectives. Hence, the PA position allows for both internal and external positions.

Moving even further towards critical hermeneutics, external perspectives are used very actively in the process of interpretation. The "objective" understanding of poverty should be made an explicit part of the interpretative process. There is currently continuous work occurring regarding the definition and redefinition of poverty, much of which might be happening at the crossroads of the two epistemological positions that Shaffer and Kanbur and Shaffer discuss. We will return to this in the next section.

The measurement of poverty within the naturalistic I/C position is based on brute (value-free) data. The definition of poverty in terms of consumption levels makes it possible to measure poverty quantitatively. Quantification is a logical, but not necessary, consequence of using brute data that are verifiable in an "objective" way. In the PA position, both qualitative and quantitative measures are possible, insofar as certain interpretations of meaning structures have to be qualitative in character. The main point is that in the PA position, poverty should not be reduced only to its quantitative dimensions, since that would deprive the poverty concept of meaning. Typically, this implies that the population coverage is more specific than in the I/C approach.

Again, it looks as though the PA and hermeneutic position might be slightly more open to interdisciplinary dialogue than the I/C position. The latter would have neo-classical economy at least as a central reference point. However, going back to the utility theory that underpins the I/C position, we may note that Bentham in the original version of this normative theory worked with the concept of utility and happiness – concepts that are not measurable inter-subjectively. The option that the revealed preferences theory provided made it necessary to move from the cardinal to the ordinal representation of utility. Further, this shift gave impetus to a host of critical reactions that argued inter-personal comparisons are not possible (utility is an internal concept, which cannot be observed objectively outside the individual, except through indicators) (Sen 1987:7ff). In other words, the problem that revealed preference theory set out to resolve is not really solved.

Based on the tensions in the problem of defining and measuring poverty, one may conclude that there is a general tension between making inter-subjective measurements versus providing understanding of what poverty means in the individual case. But rather than pitting one against the other, we may conclude that both the I/C and the PA positions share these two challenges: the search for inter-subjectivity and the simultaneous search for understanding of meaning.

In this context, the naturalist normative theory is not at all equipped to discuss or criticise *preferences,* attitudes and beliefs, since these are taken as given. What makes this position problematic is that preferences are generally not at all exogenous, but shaped through social processes. Hermeneutics, and especially critical hermeneutics, on the other hand, aims at moving beyond faulty preferences, attitudes and beliefs through self-reflection among agents and dialogue. By showing that preferences were formed in a process that did not meet the conditions for ISS, a more mature understanding may be reached (Habermas 1971:310).

The main *sources of data* in the I/C approaches are direct observation of revealed preferences through the registration of actual expenditures or indivdual's responses assembled through questionnaires. In practice, expenditures necessary to satisfy the minimum needs of dietary energy are estimated in order to arrive at the poverty level. In PA, the hermeneutic approach demands data gathered through dialogues, such as the PPA, where poor people themselves participate. This is necessary for the interpretation and understanding of what poverty means. Hence, the kind of data used is typically more non-numeric.

During the last ten to fifteen years, particularly the I/C approaches have been met with increasing doubt and criticism. This is not least due to the increased availability of improved data. Panel data allowing for more dynamic studies, as well an improved knowledge of the dimensions of ill-being other than low consumption have contributed to an intensified conceptual evolution regarding poverty. Within the discipline of economics, there has been a clear move towards dynamic rather than static models and analyses. This shift has been motivated in part by the empirical fact that changes in poverty levels are usually net changes. As people move out of poverty, a counterflow of people moving into poverty is taking place simultaneously. These dual moves may often be much larger than the net effect of the movement out of poverty. Hence, there is a need to understand both the dynamics of moving out of and into poverty (Krishna 2007).[4]

The dynamically oriented studies have encountered methodological problems, for instance the challenge of treating panel data in valid and reliable ways. In addition, they have also run into conceptual problems, for instance, the issue of how to treat time. Should time be seen as one asset among others, as part of the capability portfolio of actors? If treated in this way, lack of time is yet another constraint on agency and on the freedom to control one's own life. Alternatively, should time be seen as a dimension of dynamism, implying that time enables processes to unfold and the interplay of factors to take new routes (Addison et al. 2008)? The latter perspective opens the way for a larger discussion about static versus dynamic analyses, where the systematic and methodological inclusion of dynamic elements, like time, learning or institutions, tends to link the discipline of economics more closely to other social science disciplines (Ekeland 2009).

The *objective* of the naturalist position is to describe and explain social reality in correct ways. Both descriptions and explanations should be value neutral: descriptions must not prescribe what ought to be, explanations must not evaluate social phenomena. Hence, it

---

4. The fact that people move in and out of poverty simultaneously in most cases implies as well that the assumption made in the pro-poor growth discussion that poverty reduction follows from economic growth may need to be questioned.

is important in this position to respect consumer preferences as given, and to keep factual descriptions unbiased. The sources of ill-being or poverty are, according to this position, inadequate private consumption of essential goods and services. Hence, explanations of poverty centre on the reasons for this missing consumption. In PA, the objective of research is to understand the meaning of poverty. False consciousness should be revealed through self-reflection and dialogue. This should lead to emancipation. Explanations are helpful, but will necessarily include evaluation. In particular, the claims to validity posed by speakers should be evaluated. According to this position, the sources of poverty go beyond consumption. Typical explanations of poverty would thus include income and non-income sources of entitlements, social relations of reproduction, production and exchange, employment conditions, autonomy, self-respect and others.

Even if there is an essential tension between these two objectives, we may, both here as well as in the other areas discussed, see openings for work that transcends the I/C and PA positions on epistemology, normative theory and methods.

1.5 Emerging perspectives

We strongly agree with Shaffer (1996) and Kanbur and Shaffer (2005) that differences at the level of epistemology and normative theory are essential in every discussion of poverty concepts, measurement, understanding and explanation. However, where we differ is on the conclusion as to the effects these differences might have on the prospects for future cross-disciplinary work on poverty. As we have mentioned briefly in relation to all the points discussed above, there are possibilities to move beyond the differences and bridge the philosophical divides. These are by no means simple tasks, but there are promising openings that Kanbur and Shaffer have not emphasised enough.

A route that is increasingly being taken is one that moves from the unidimensionality of poverty towards multidimensionality. Material poverty was in a way already broadened and complemented in the 1970s with the introduction of the basic needs concept. However, it is during the 1990s and beyond that multidimensionality has more thoroughly gained ground (Sen 1999). Insights about multiple situations of deprivation have driven this shift. Deprivation in terms of health or disempowerment or other important aspects of poverty may have different impacts from deprivation in terms of income or consumption (Alkire and Foster 2008:1).

So far, the multidimensional drive has probably been strongest within the field of development economics. Criticism from within the discipline has pointed to the weaknesses of quantitative methods in getting at the central aspects of poverty dynamics. Hence, awareness has grown that cross-disciplinary research is needed. This has been paralleled by a discussion of the limitations of aggregated quantitative methods, such as cross-country regressions, and the need to establish clearer links between macro- and micro theory and analysis (Besley and Burgess 2002; Jerven 2009). Thus, leading economists have over the last decade involved themselves in discussions about methodological cross-fertilisation and multidisciplinary collabouration.[5]

---

5. The prime example is the Q-Squared project, which combines qualitative and quantitative methods and is hosted by the University of Toronto. This has resulted in numerous seminars and working papers on methodological and multidisciplinary issues related to research on poverty: http://www.q-squared.ca/

The multidimensional turn has brought with it a number of problems (OPHI 2007);

i)   The lack of, or poor quality of, data particularly on aspects other than income or consumption is an obvious weakness. It would take major investments by governments and international actors to rectify this, implying that improved measures will take some time to emerge. The use of panel data and re-surveying is encouraged in trying to get at dynamic processes. However, such data are costly to produce and demand patience on the part of respondents. For instance, to track the movement of a particular sample over time is both difficult and costly.

ii) The problem of finding relevant indicators of, or operationalising such dimensions of poverty as informal employment, agency and empowerment, physical safety, or the ability to go without shame is another difficulty. When should one be satisfied with the list of factors to include in a poverty measurement? And what would other possible candidates be? The choice of dimensions that represent valuable capabilities is a normative choice. However, there are clear limitations to what normative theory can provide for the choice of indicators for each dimension. Hence, some kind of combination between normative theory and empirical studies is needed for such a selection.

iii) A closely related problem concerns what relative importance, or what weight, the various dimensions of the multidimensional poverty concept should be given. Problems related to validity are involved. Statistical methods, such as factorial analysis and participatory rankings of well-being, may not provide similar conclusions. As well, there are problems with reliability: participatory rankings may not arrive at the same concept of poverty from one place to another.

iv) Establishing the interconnectedness between various dimensions is another complication. Some capabilities have both intrinsic and instrumental value in that they drive other capabilities (for instance, education may be a value in itself, providing self-esteem, but at the same time important in increasing employment): the interconnectedness is essential and searching for endogeneity becomes important.

v)   The tendency for preferences and perceptions of subjective dimensions to be adapted through processes emerging from membership of various and often overlapping groups. This problem refers to larger issues of methodological individualism and the formation of preferences either through social processes or through independent individual choices, which we have touched on above.

With all these difficulties in mind, Foster and Alkire (2007), and more widely the Oxford Poverty and Human Development Initiative, OPHI, have embarked on the endeavour to develop tools that should make the capability approach inter-subjectively measurable, and at the same time capture the meaning of poverty. They work with quantitative methods and econometric tools, but even if they start from a naturalist or empiricist perspective, they try to bridge to other perspectives as well. What they have initially focused on are the missing dimensions in the poverty concept, and developing tools for measuring many dimensions simultaneously.

The tools they have constructed make it possible to use both ordinal and cardinal data. (Alkire and Foster 2008:10). This is important since it allows for working with data that is more readily available, and even for measuring dimensions that are more difficult to operationalise. The Alkire-Foster (A-F) tool for measuring multidimensional poverty operates in 12 separate steps. An underlying idea is to separate the process of identifying who is poor from the process of aggregating the measures into an overall indicator of poverty. Furthermore, the purpose is to avoid a measure that either portrays people as poor if they are deprived in only one dimension, or portrays them as poor only if they are deprived in all dimensions.

The 12-step tool can briefly be described as follows. When the dimensions and indicators of poverty are chosen, separate poverty lines are set out for each dimension. These are used as cutoffs, according to agreed criteria. People can be poor in one dimension or more. These dimensions can then be weighted differently when the numbers of deprivations are added together. Following this, a second cutoff level is set, where it is decided in how many dimensions a person needs to be deprived in order to be classified as poor. On the basis of this poverty headcount, the average poverty gap as well as the adjusted headcount can be calculated (Alkire and Foster 2007:4f). The measure can then be disaggregated by group or by the different dimensions. This makes the method useful as a planning and policy tool.

Already, this extremely brief synopsis of the A-F tool indicates that there are a number of steps that potentially involve dialogue and interpretation in the definition of what poverty is, and who is poor. Even if it works primarily with quantitative data, and comes from an empiricist tradition, this tool makes possible bridges to hermeneutics and the participatory approach. The PPA and other methods that are preferred by PA may be used at various stages in the process of defining and measuring multidimensional poverty.

The participatory approach has made many important contributions. It provides for the inclusion of context as well as meaning, which are essential elements for deeper understanding. However, one basic weakness with PA is that inter-subjectivity tends to get lost in the process. This implies that comparisons across societies and countries are rendered, if not impossible, at least very difficult and potentially misleading. Cross-country and cross-society comparisons are, after all, essential for policy relevance, and for putting knowledge to practical use. Potentially, however, there is another and possibly more serious problem with participatory methods, which is particularly problematic in relation to processes of deprivation. People may exhibit "adaptive preferences" (Nussbaum 2006:73), which implies that the preferences they hold have already been shaped and curbed by deprivations they are subject to. If something is seen as not being within reach, not possible to achieve for a person who perceives of her- /himself in a particular category or position, preferences are regularly adjusted to be in the realm of the realistic – people adjust their preferences to what they think they can achieve. Such processes of self-censorship are often practised, for instance, by women, who might, due to social conventions, have lower aspirations than their male counterparts. It is difficult to get information on the prevalence of adaptive preferences through participatory research methods, because these methods explicitly aim at mapping expressed preferences.

Compare across individuals and societies

In an attempt to move beyond this weakness of participatory methods, Martha Nussbaum's version of the capability approach (ibid. 76ff) reintroduces inter-subjectivity in a way that aims at capturing a more basic human level. This is done in a way that does not necessarily exclude the possibility of understanding poverty in a contextual way. Nussbaum describes an open-ended list of ten central human capabilities. This list is not exhaustive and can change, but is an attempt at summarising what human life is about. When people are deprived of one or more of these capabilities, they will be characterised as poor:

1. Life – being able to live a worthy life of normal length;
2. Bodily health – to be adequately nourished, sheltered and have good health, including reproductive;
3. Bodily integrity – being able to move around freely and securely, having choice in matters of reproduction and sexual satisfaction;
4. Senses, imagination and thought – to be able to use the senses, imagine, think and reason in a truly human way based on education; using imagination and thought in producing work and events of one's own choice; using one's mind in ways protected by freedom of expression;
5. Emotions – to be able to attach to things and people, to love, to grieve, to experience longing, gratitude and justified anger;
6. Practical reason – to be able to form a conception of the good and to critically reflect on the planning of one's own life;
7. Affiliation – being able to live with and towards others, recognise and show concern for other human beings and engage in various forms of social interaction; having the social bases of self-respect and non-humiliation; being able to be treated as a dignified being whose worth is equal to that of others, which includes nondiscrimination;
8. Other species – being able to live with concern for and in relation to animals, plants and the world of nature;
9. Play – being able to laugh, to play and enjoy recreational activities; and
10. Control over one's environment – being able to participate in political choices that govern one's life; to hold property and have property rights on an equal basis with others; have the right to seek employment on an equal basis with others and to work as a human being.

To move from this list to a definition and measure of poverty, the 12-step measuring tool developed by Alkire and Foster may be used. This implies that the definition of what poverty is would be open to dialogue, and that deprivation in more than one of the proposed dimensions above would have to be weighed against the others.

Nussbaum's main argument is that a list is needed to make sure that the wrong capabilities are not prioritised. Some freedoms limit others, some freedoms are bad and some freedoms are more important than others, she argues. Hence commitments about substance are necessary (Nussbaum, 2003). Lists such as hers may always be criticised for not capturing what is particular to some societies, or for presenting central capabilities in ways that turn out to be unbalanced in relation to actual situations. Therefore, she explicitly welcomes criticism and presents her list as a proposal. And criticism is exactly what has met her list. As Amartya Sen writes: "The problem is not with listing important capabilities, but with insisting on one predetermined canonical list of capabilities, chosen by theorists without any general social discussion or public reasoning" (Sen 2004:77). To Sen, the lack of capabilities can never be the same in all societies all the time. Furthermore, the capabilities need also to be understood, formulated and valued by citizens. Anything else would be a denial of democracy and a misunderstanding of what pure theory might do, he claims (ibid., p. 78ff). Another of Sen's arguments against a canonical list is that one and the same list cannot be used for all different evaluative purposes that occur in practice. The selection of capabilities must be tailored to the task at hand. Taking such positions, Sen lines himself up with the position taken by hermeneutics, with its emphasis on deliberative processes and discursive normative theory.

A more principled view on the choice of what capabilities to include in the poverty definition is taken by Sabina Alkire. She refers to Ingrid Robeyns in suggesting four principles for the selection of capabilities:

i)   Explicit formulation of and argumentation for the selection;
ii) Justification of the method used in generating the list of capabilities;
iii) A two-stage process that differentiates between the ideal and the feasible; and
iv) The inclusion of all dimensions that are important.

In applying criteria that require the researcher to formulate a list of capabilities through a process that is open to questioning, Alkire and Robeyns place themselves somewhere in between the positions taken by Nussbaum and Sen. This is also a position in between the naturalistic and the hermeneutic positions, in the sense that it opens up the possibility to combine brute data with deliberative processes. In this sense, it provides an opening for a middle way.

1.6 A third way emerging

The capability approach (CA) is in itself a normative framework, evaluating social situations according to the amount of freedom people have to promote the functionings they value and have reason to value. The CA may utilise methodologies and analytical techniques of all kinds, and it may use both quantitative and qualitative data gathered from the full range of sources. It is described as a "… framework that researchers can draw on in order to utilize diverse approaches to multidimensional poverty and well-being in a concerted and conceptually coherent fashion" (Alkire, 2008:2).

In describing the theoretical underpinnings of the approach, Nussbaum and Sen are in agreement that the capability approach has been developed as an alternative to utilitarianism (Nussbaum 2006: 408f; Sen 2009:19, 69f). While utilitarianism focuses on the satisfaction of various goals, it misses the central role of agency, which occurs on Nussbaum's list above. In Nussbaum's view, it is not enough to achieve satisfaction without choice and activity. In this way, utilitarianism might play down the importance of democratic choice, as well as agency.

CA has its roots in the social contract theory[6] and builds on many of its principles. However, it is simultaneously in opposition to this theory when it comes to the principle of mutual advantage as the basis for social cooperation. CA presupposes more of the moral sentiments than contractual theory does. Where contractual theories are parsimonious, in

6. Social contract theory was developed by David Hume, John Locke, Immanuel Kant and others. Its best-known current version is probably the theory of justice developed by John Rawls (1971). The basic idea is that individuals agree to be part of a society and to collaaburate with a state on the basis of an implicit agreement that they will in some way gain from this.

the sense that they claim that collabouration in society is possible not because of people's benevolence but because everyone benefits from cooperation, the capability approach demands more from human beings (Nussbaum, 2006: 408f). This is a potential weakness of CA. Despite this, it provides a promising way forward by opening up perspectives that include both qualitative understanding and inter-subjectivity. The attempt aims at establishing functions of human life that are valid across cultures and societies, and thus may be the basis for cross-societal and cross-individual comparisons and assessments.

Even so, and even if CA is correctly described as a normative *framework*, it is possible to take different positions within CA in relation to normative *theory*. This conclusion may be drawn from the debate between Nussbaum and Sen referred to above over the list of capabilities. While Nussbaum takes an inter-subjective and unitary normative position, Sen aligns himself with the position of discursive normative theory, with its emphasis on deliberative participation. Still, both are applying the same normative framework to the study of poverty.

One might wonder what, if anything, will have been gained if the kinds of divergent positions that Kanbur and Shaffer point to between the naturalists and hermeneutics are now taken by the main proponents of a newer and trans-boundary approach such as CA? There are in fact gains. The largest gain is arguably that there is now a debate where both the issue of inter-subjective comparison and the issue of the understanding of meaning of poverty are seen as real problems, at the same level of importance. Regardless of position, everyone must today deal with these challenges and the trade-off between them. Another important gain is that within the CA tradition all kinds of methods and data can be used interchangeably, depending on what issues are raised and what questions asked.

But, what about the utilitarian tradition with its revealed preference theory and its naturalist position, then? Both Nussbaum and Sen take the explicit position that the CA was developed as an alternative to utilitarianism. Hence, CA can hardly be claimed to be a bridge to those kinds of positions. This being so, one might still recall that in the earlier version of utilitarian theory, Bentham and others worked with the "happiness" concept, which is not inter-subjectively quantifiable. As well, when the revealed preference theory with the money metric was developed, this met with the reaction that inter-personal comparisons of well-being were not possible (Sen 1987:7ff). As we have reported, there has over recent years been a continuing debate about the need for multidimensionality and cross-disciplinary approaches to poverty studies. Many economists, coming from the utilitarian and naturalist tradition, have taken an active part in this, and been among the key driving forces behind it. Hence, even if not all will choose to take part in it, the emergence of the capability approach to the study of well-being and poverty provides a common framework and arena. This makes it possible to find common epistemological ground and work with possible trade-offs between inter-subjective comparisons and the understanding of meaning; to find common normative positions; to combine all sorts of methodologies and to utilise different sets of data.

1.7 Conclusion

This essay has described the conceptual debate about poverty and how poverty should be defined and measured. This description builds on two major philosophical traditions, which have resulted in two distinct approaches to the definition and measurement of poverty: the income/consumption approach and the participative approach. We have moved on to argue that the fairly recent emergence of the capability approach to the understanding and study of poverty provides middle ground between these two positions. Furthermore, the capability approach makes it possible to use a multitude of methods and data. It is thus a useful platform for moving in the warranted direction of further multidisciplinary, multidimensional and dynamic approaches to the study of poverty.

It is clear that many and fundamental lines of division first and foremost between economics and anthropology remain: the formalist-substantivist debate, differing perceptions of autonomy versus embeddedness, outcomes versus process, parsimony versus complexity – these are just some of the lines of division (Bardhan and Ray 2006). However, this is not the place for such debates. The current discussion is intended to illustrate where the most important lines of division for the study of poverty lie. We agree with Kanbur and Shaffer that differences of epistemology and normative theory are of fundamental importance in describing and analysing what separates various positions on the definition, measurement and explanation of poverty. We further agree that these differences have not been highlighted enough in the past.

However, we do not agree that such differences necessarily need to remain. The evolution of the capability approach opens up possibilities to bridge the epistemological and normative barriers. This will not happen in a way that abandons the differences once and for all. Rather, the capability approach provides an arena where such differences can be discussed. Instead of being fundamental lines of division, tensions between inter-subjective measurement and contextual understanding, as well as between externally justified and internally adaptive preferences may be treated as the trade-offs that they are. No-one can escape such difficulties any longer by hiding away in any single epistemological corner.

REFERENCES

Addison, T., D. Hulme and R. Kanbur, 2008: "Poverty Dynamics: Measurement and Understanding from an Interdisciplinary Perspective", BWPI Working Paper 19, University of Manchester.

Alkire, S., 2008: "Choosing Dimensions; The Capability Approach and Multidimensional Poverty", Munich Personal RePEc Archive Paper No 8862, Munich.

Alkire, S. and J. Foster, 2008: "Counting and Multidimensional Poverty", Working Paper 7, Oxford Poverty and Human Development Initiative, Queen Elizabeth House, Oxford University.

Anderson, D. and V. Broch-Due, 1999: *The Poor are Not Us – Poverty and Pastoralism*. Oxford: James Currey; Nairobi: EAEP; and Athens: Ohio University Press.

Bardhan, P. and I. Ray, 2006: "Methodological Approaches in Economics and Anthropology", Q-Squared Working Paper 17, University of Toronto.

Bentham, J., (1789) 1948: *The Principles of Morals and Legislation*. New York: Haffner Press.

Berry, S., 1985: *Fathers Work for their Sons*. Berkeley: University of California Press.

—, 1993: *No Condition is Permanent*. Madison University of Wisconsin Press.

Besley, T. and R. Burgess, 2002: "Redistribution, Growth and Poverty Reduction", LSE (mimeo) London.

Chambers, R., 2006: "What is Poverty? Who asks? Who answers? in *Poverty in Focus*, UNDP International Poverty Centre, December 2006.

Ehrenpreis, D., 2009: "Poverty – What it is and what to do about it —Ideas and Policies in the International Community and in Swedish Development Cooperation" (mimeo).

Ekeland, 2009: "Havelmoo – a low key heterodox?" (mimeo).

Foster, J., J. Greer and E. Thorbecke, 1984: "A Class of Decomposable Poverty Measures", *Econometrica* 52(3).

Gasper, D.R., 1996: "Needs and Basic Needs: A Clarification of Meanings, Levels and Different Streams of Work", Working Paper 210, Institute of Social Studies, The Hague, The Netherlands.

Giddens, A., 1976: *New Rules of Sociological Method*. London: Hutchinson.

Guillaumont, P., S. Guillaumont and J.F. Brun, 1999: "How Instability Lowers African Growth", *Journal of African Economies* 8(17):87-107.

Habermas, J., 1971: *Knowledge and Human Interests*. Boston: Beacon Press.

–, 1979: *Communication and the Evolution of Society*. London: Hellemann Educational Books.

–, 1990: *Moral Consciousness and Communicative Action*. Cambridge MA: MIT Press.

Hårsmar, M., 2004: "Heavy Clouds but No Rain – Agricultural Growth Theories and Peasant Strategies on the Mossi Plateau, Burkina Faso", Dissertation Agraria 439, Swedish University of Agricultural Sciences, Uppsala.

Kalwij, A. and A. Vershoor, 2007: "Not by Growth Alone: The Role of the Distribution of Income in Regional Diversity in Poverty Reduction", *European Economic Review* 51(4):805-29.

Kanbur, R. and P. Shaffer, 2005: "Epistemology, Normative Theory and Poverty Analysis: Implications for Q-Squared in Practice", Working Paper 2, Q-Squared, University of Toronto.

Krishna, A., 2007: "Escaping Poverty and Becoming Poor in Three States of India, with Additional Evidence from Kenya, Uganda and Peru", in Narayan, D. and P. Patesch (eds): *Moving Out of Poverty – Cross-Disciplinary Perspectives on Mobility*. London: Palgrave; Washington DC: World Bank.

Kristensson Uggla, B., 2002: "Slaget om verkligheten – filosofi, omvärldsanalys, tolkning", Symposion, Lund.

Lesamana, J. A.M., 2009: "Transition from Subsistence to Monetary Economy – A Counter Discource to Mainstream Development Strategies", Master's Thesis, Development Management, University of Agder, Kristiansand.

Locke, J. 1847 (1689): "An Essay Concerning Human Understanding". Pittsburgh: Kay and Troutman (digitalized by Google Books).

Lübcke, P., 1988: "Filiosofilexikonet". Stockholm: Forum.

Nussbaum, M.C., 2003: "Capabilities as Fundamental Entitlements: Sen and Social Justice", *Feminist Economics* 9(2/3).

–, 2006: *Frontiers of Justice – Disability, Nationality, Species Membership*. Cambridge MA: Belknap/ Harvard University Press.

OPHI, 2007: "Annex: OPHI Research Agenda Details", Queen Elizabeth House, Oxford University.

Ravallion, M. 2001: "Growth, Inequality and Poverty: Looking Beyond Averages", *World Development* 29 (11):1803-15.

Ravallion, M., S. Chen and P. Sangraula, 2008: "Dollar a Day Revisited" (mimeo). Washington DC.: World Bank.

Rawls, J., 1971: *A Theory of Justice*. Cambridge MA: Harvard University Press.

Robeyns, I., 2003: "Sen's Capability Approach and Gender Inequality: Selecting Relevant Capabilities", *Feminist Economics* 9.

–, 2005: "Assessing Global Poverty and Inequality: Income Resources and Capability" in C. Barry and T. Pogge (eds): *Global Institutions and Responsibilities – Achieving Global Justice*. Oxford: Blackwell.

Rosenberg, A., 1988: *Philosophy of Social Science*. Boulder CO: Westview.

Ruggeri Laderchi, C., R. Saith and F. Stewart, 2006: "Does the Definition of Poverty Matter? - Comparing four approaches" in *Poverty in Focus*, UNDP International Poverty Centre, December 2006.

Sen, A.K., 1987: *The Standard of Living*. Cambridge: Cambridge University Press.

–, 1999: *Development as Freedom*. Oxford/ New York: Oxford University Press.

–, 2004: "Capabilities, Lists and Public Reason: Continuing the Conversation", *Feminist Economics* 10 (3).

–, 2009: *The Idea of Justice*. London: Allen Lane.

Shaffer, P., 1996: "Beneath the Poverty Debate – Some Issues", *IDS Bulletin* 27(1), IDS, University of Sussex, Brighton.

–, 1998: "Gender, Poverty and Deprivation: Evidence from the Republic of Guinea", *World Development* 26(12):2119-35.

Son, H. and N. Kakwani, 2006: "Global Estimates of Pro-Poor Growth", IPC Working Paper Series 31, IPC, Brazil.

Taylor, C., 1985: *Philosophy and the Human Sciences: Philosophical Papers*, vol. II. Cambridge: Cambridge University Press.

Tilly, C., 2007: "Poverty and the Politics of Exclusion" in Narayan, D. and P. Patesch (eds): *Moving Out of Poverty – Cross-Disciplinary Perspectives on Mobility*. London: Palgrave; Wahsington DC: World Bank.

von Wright, G.H., 1971: *Explanation and Understanding.* London: Routledge and Kegan Paul.
World Bank, 2007: *Africa Development Indicators,* Washington DC.
–, 2008: *Poverty Data – A Supplement to World Development Indicators 2008,* Washington DC.

2. Living on the brink – poverty patterns compared

2.1 Introduction

The 1990s were characterised by economic adjustment in many parts of sub-Saharan Africa (SSA). This was a period of contested economic reform, followed by what turned out to be a period of unprecedentedly high economic growth in many countries in the region during the first decade of the 21st century. On the macroeconomic front, stabilisation and balance were much improved and international initiatives for debt reduction further helped to enhance the economic outlook. Increasing numbers of African leaders stressed the importance of macroeconomic stability and applied reforms requested by international financial institutions. However, economic growth and opportunities did not translate into poverty reduction at a level that had been hoped for.[7] This was the case, even though minor improvements may be noted in most of those SSA countries where poverty statistics are available and in the region as a whole (World Bank 2008:11 and 16f). Simultaneously, inequality has increased in many cases. Closer examination reveals that important net changes in poverty levels and patterns have taken place, but these changes have still to be fully analysed.

Burkina Faso and Tanzania are two countries in SSA where economic reforms were followed by per capita economic growth from the 1990s onwards. Both countries may also be cases where poverty dynamics need to be better analysed and understood. Important work has been done in this regard. However, a comparison between two such cases may yield important wider lessons, both in terms of what the relevant scope of study is and of the lessons that may be valid for other SSA countries.

2.2 Purpose and methodology

The purpose of this study is to describe current poverty dynamics in two African countries in order to identify where significant poverty reduction is taking place, and where poverty is increasing. Hypotheses as to why these dynamics are evident will be formulated and discussed. A consideration of some of the potential for and limitations on further poverty reduction will also be provided.

The reasons for selecting Tanzania and Burkina Faso are that both have undertaken macroeconomic reforms during the 1990s, for which they have received positive assessments from international financial institutions; both have experienced rapid per capita economic growth over a number of years; but also because both have an economic structure representative of a larger number of African countries. Both are heavily dependent on agriculture, while at the same time trying to make inroads into the service and manufacturing sectors. Their levels of technological development are comparable. As we will see, these two countries share with SSA countries in general a situation where economic growth is a weak factor in explaining variance in poverty levels. In this respect, SSA countries differ from other comparable countries.

In Burkina Faso and Tanzania, it is furthermore the case that data are relatively more available than in some other African countries, and hence that substantial amounts of research have been undertaken in both countries. The potential for somewhat more thorough analyses is therefore present in these cases.

---

7. Personal communication with Shanta Devarajan, chief economist, Africa department, World Bank, 21 March 2010. See also Ravallion (2010) and Fosu (2009).

The two countries differ in a number of ways: in terms of colonial history – one a former French colony, and the other a former German/British colony; in the rate of population growth (3.1 percent/annum BF, 2.1 percent/annum Tz; US Census Bureau 2009); and also in terms of natural resources, with Tanzania having the higher potential of the two.

Since the similarities in relevant areas are greater and wider than the differences between these countries, the case selection is closest to the "most similar case" selection method, if any. This method may be used to identify important possible factors driving differences in poverty outcomes, should these belong to the category of factors that differs between the cases. However, the ambition in this section is not to make causal inferences, but rather to provide an in-depth description of the pattern of poverty that has emerged over roughly the last decade.

As discussed in the previous article, poverty should be studied in a multidimensional way. However, given the data availability, we must still focus on the material aspects of poverty, primarily measured in monetary terms, with the incidence, depth and severity of poverty being measured using the Foster, Greer, Thorbecke (FGT 1984) approach. This is a drawback, in that our understanding of poverty dynamics will be limited. There are other aspects of poverty that would have made possible a broader understanding of the factors causing poverty. However, for the time being we will have to live with this limitation. The methodological contribution this study will make is rather to test what may be gained from enhanced cross-disciplinary approaches and from the combination of various methods of data-gathering.

The general methodology applied in this study is to start from current quantitative analyses of poverty and vulnerability, and describe how these factors have evolved over the last approximately fifteen years in the two countries. This description will build on a number of recent studies. Patterns emerging from such studies will then be dealt with by referring to qualitative studies of the population groups that have either moved out of, or fallen into poverty in these two countries. By examining livelihoods of the affected people in greater depth, and by combining quantitative and qualitative information, a deeper understanding of prevailing poverty dynamics may be achieved.

As the study shows, a central concept is vulnerability. This refers to the likelihood that a household will experience a future loss of welfare. Such risk is sometimes weighted by the scale of the expected welfare loss, but it may also be calculated as the risk as such. Heitzman et al. (2002) discuss a risk chain, which includes the risk or uncertainty; the available options for managing risks; and the outcome in terms of welfare loss. A vulnerable household is one that is both exposed to risks and is unable to respond adequately to such risks. Alternatively, a household may be classified as vulnerable if it has a high probability of ending up in poverty, which is the ultimate effect of not having the appropriate abilities to respond to risk (Lachaud 2002). The main difference between these two approaches is the way vulnerability is measured, calculated or estimated. There is no consensus on how to measure vulnerability. Whereas one approach associates vulnerability with low expected utility, the other (i.e., Lachaud) links it to high expected poverty. The latter approach will be used in this study.

2.3 Economic growth and poverty in sub-Saharan Africa

Discussions have arisen in Burkina Faso and in Tanzania as to why poverty has remained unexpectedly stable during periods of extended per capita economic growth. Why did poverty not decrease more? In Burkina Faso, the phenomenon has been labelled the "Burkinabé growth-poverty paradox", since inequality also remained stable during this period of growth, according to official statistics. How come economic growth resulted in neither poverty reduction nor increased inequality? Obviously, something must be wrong with the measurements. But is this only a data problem, or are underlying patterns of growth and poverty following unexpected paths? Furthermore, are such debates relevant to something that is peculiar to just these two countries, or are we observing a more widespread phenomenon?

Focusing particularly on SSA, Fosu (2009) concludes that the degree of poverty responsiveness to growth is lower in SSA than in other developing regions. In addition, he finds that this holds for all three of the poverty measures he uses (headcount, gap and squared gap). He finds the poverty elasticity of growth to be nearly three times as high for countries outside SSA, as compared with SSA.[8] For the period 1977-2004, Fosu (ibid.:735) estimates poverty elasticity in SSA to be between 1.123 and -1.154 based on the 1 US$/day measure of poverty. The variation in his result depends on which model is used. Christiaensen et al. (2003) estimate the poverty elasticity of growth to be -0.89 for eight countries in SSA during the 1990s. Still, such levels of elasticity are substantially lower than estimates for developing economies in general. As a comparison, Ravallion (2001) estimated these to be -2.5 as an average for 47 developing countries during the 1980s and 1990s. Fosu estimated poverty elasticity for his comparative group of non-SSA countries to be between -2.87 to -3.25. He further notes that the differences in poverty elasticity between countries in SSA and elsewhere are largest in the headcount measure of poverty. When the poverty gap and squared gap are calculated, differences in elasticity are smaller.

Interestingly, Fosu (ibid.:734) shows that higher levels of inequality may explain part of this difference between countries in SSA and other developing countries. Income-growth poverty elasticity decreases with rising inequality. As well, initial inequality matters: higher initial inequality reduces the rate at which growth in income leads to reductions in poverty. Since inequality is higher in SSA than in the control group of non-SSA countries, economic growth would lead to less poverty reduction there.

However, the inequality hypothesis has been questioned by Ravallion (2010), who also dwells on the issue of why poverty reduction is faster in some of the less poor countries than in the poorest. His starting point is that the poorer a country is, the faster economic growth should be, according to economic theory. Since additional economic growth would lead to reductions in poverty, poverty reductions should be faster in poorer countries. Why is there then evidence to the contrary? His answer is that there is also an opposing effect stemming from the higher initial poverty level that leads to lower economic growth. Which one of these two factors dominates is an empirical question.

With the help of a new data set based on household surveys from almost 100 developing countries conducted from 1980 onwards, Ravallion goes on to test these issues. Is it inequality, the presence of a middle class, or poverty that causes poverty reduction to be slower? Testing this is difficult, since the definitions of inequality, poverty and the middle class are all in monetary terms. Hence, there is a great risk that these variables reflect similar or identical dynamics. Nevertheless, Ravallion finds that it is the initial level of poverty that leads to lower rates of poverty reduction. This occurs through two different channels: i) a direct adverse effect, where high levels of poverty lead to lower rates of growth; ii) an indirect effect, where economic growth implies lower reductions in poverty in countries with high initial poverty levels. Contrary to Fosu's results, Ravallion registered no separate effects from inequality when controlling for initial poverty levels (ibid.:29f).

---

8. Similar differences, albeit at a lower scale, were also found by Kalwij and Verschoor 2007:818.

That SSA is different from other developing regions has been discussed and argued for a long time. In the latter half of the 1990s, the attempts to explain a statistically significant Africa dummy variable in models of what was driving economic growth were perhaps most intense (Easterly and Levine 1997; Guillaumont et al. 1999; Kenny and Syrquin 1999). A vast number of variables have been proposed and tested, but the issue has not been finally resolved (Christiaensen et al. 2003). In his critique of the whole literature on the African growth dummy, Jerven (2009) emphasises the fact that the period of rapid growth in the 1960s and early 1970s has been lumped together with the period of retrogression in the late 1970s and 1980s. During the first of these two periods, African economies grew at the same rate as the world average. The African dummy has nothing to tell us about why Africa first grew and then regressed. The period of rapid economic growth in the first decade of the 21st century is also left unexplained when variables that reflect long-term "character flaws" in the African continent are applied as explanations.

In estimating the influence of poverty on economic growth, Ravallion (2010:23) found no significant regional effect for SSA. His interpretation is that the African dummy disappears when controlling for initial levels of poverty. Fosu (2009), on the other hand, concluded that levels of poverty elasticity to growth were clearly lower in SSA than elsewhere. He based this on a slightly smaller sample of countries than Ravaillon, but a longer period. Another difference is that Ravallion tested for an Africa dummy, while Fosu isolated SSA as the differing unit. Given the harsh critique of cross-country regressions on methodological and empirical grounds (Jerven 2009; Kenny and Williams 2001), we should be careful about drawing firm conclusions from these two studies. Nevertheless, there seems to be agreement that poverty reduction in SSA is not occurring at the same rate as it is in other developing countries. Regardless of whether it is high levels of initial poverty or some Africa-specific factor that causes this, it is relevant to dig deeper into questions of economic growth and poverty reduction at national and sub-national levels. What we find in Burkina Faso and Tanzania might also be relevant for other countries. The relationship between growth and poverty is at least for a substantial number of SSA countries different from what it is in countries in other parts of the developing world.

2.4 Burkina Faso

Available data on poverty in Burkina Faso come from three broad household surveys, undertaken in 1994-95, 1998 and 2003 respectively (*Enquêtes prioritaires* I, II and III). Estimations in these surveys are based on interviews with approximately 8,500 households on each occasion, spread over the nation and chosen randomly. More than five years have passed since the last of these major household surveys was undertaken. A new survey was expected during the second half of 2009, but the results will not be compiled until probably a year later.

Generally, the incidence of poverty is remarkably similar among the three surveys: 44.5 percent of the total population of the country lived under the monetary poverty line in 1994, whereas 45.3 percent did in 1998 and 46.4 percent in 2003.[9] The major part of this poverty, over 90 percent, is rural, even though the share of urban poverty has risen substantially. This lack of change in poverty levels has occurred despite the fact that Burkina Faso

---

9. Calculated as percentages of households, the share of poor are 34.5, 34.6 and 37.5 percent. The poverty line used is defined nationally. It is substantially lower than the poverty line that the World Bank uses as an international standard, the US$ 1.25/day poverty line. The latter is calculated as a mean of all the different national poverty lines in developing countries (Ravallion et al. 2008). The difference between the Burkina Faso poverty line and the US$ 1.25/day line thus reflects the fact that Burkina Faso is among the poorest countries in the world. The same applies for the poverty line used in Tanzania.

experienced economic growth over the whole period studied. Between 1994 and 1998, GDP increased on average by 4.5 percent annually, and over 1996-2006 it reached 4.8 percent as an annual average (Bourdet and Thiombiano 2009).

However, the official poverty figures are highly contested. Given that Burkina Faso has seen high economic growth during this period, such stability in the incidence of poverty should mean increasing inequality, as we discussed above. This is particularly so since the most rapid growth occurred in the service sector, which is mainly based in urban areas, whereas urban poverty actually increased (ibid.:27f). But inequality, as measured by the Gini coefficient, has also stayed constant, at 0.46 as a national average in all three of the relevant years, according to official estimates. It is this contradiction that has been referred to as the "Burkinabé growth-poverty paradox".

In trying to resolve this paradox, Grimm-Günther (2006) criticised changes that were made between the three surveys in defining the poverty lines, calculating household expenditures and, to a lesser extent, in survey design. The single factor having the largest adverse impact on the end results was a recalculation made in the 1998 survey only, whereby all household expenditures were inflated by a factor of 12.5 percent. This recalculation was not generally known of until six years later (Tesulic 2004). According to reports, the change was introduced by the National Statistics Institute, INSD, on the direct advice of the World Bank in order for the results in the survey to match the results achieved from macro-level national accounts. This practice is used in other countries, for instance India. However, the across-the-board increase of expenditures was criticised by Grimm-Günther as well as others (Lachaud 2005; Tesulic 2004), who claimed that it is not reasonable to equate expenditure patterns in rural and urban settings. Furthermore, statistics on national economic growth are imprecise in countries where large parts of the economy are in the informal sphere, and hence are difficult to measure. Increased formalisation of the economy would in such cases automatically contribute to increasing levels of GDP. On balance, the conclusion that estimates from the micro-level are less credible than estimates from the macro-level seems unsubstantiated because of these and other factors.

Furthermore, Grimm-Günther questioned the non-inclusion of shadow rents for housing, mainly in the 1994 survey, but partly also in the other surveys; the inclusion of other capital assets in some, but not all the surveys; differences in the length of periods for the calculation of expenditures; as well as differences in what period of the year the surveys were undertaken. Based on this critique, Grimm-Günther made their own estimates of the poverty lines for the survey years, and following this, of the incidence of poverty. According to their results, the incidence of poverty followed an inverted U-shape, with an increase between 1994 and 1998 and a fall in poverty incidence thereafter. By introducing these changes in the statistics, they managed to resolve the growth-poverty paradox.

By contrast, Lauchaud argued that the paradox could also have been caused by the differences appearing basically because the studies were undertaken at macro- and micro-levels respectively. These levels do not necessarily correspond. Hence, he questioned most of the recalculation done by Grimm-Günther, while agreeing with them that the 12.5 percent increase in the household expenditures in the 1998 survey had to be discounted.

The various results in terms of poverty incidence (p_0 in the FGT denotation), depth (p_1) and severity (p_2) that emerged from the different approaches are shown in the following table:

Mats Hårsmar

	1994			1998			2003		
INSD 1994, 1998, 2003: Lachaud 2001, 2003									
	incid.	depth	severity	incid.	depth	severity	Incid.	depth	severity
Total	0,445	0,139	0,060	0,453	0,137	0,059	0,464	0,156	0,071
Rural	0,510	0,161	0,070	0,510	0,157	0,068	0,523	0,179	0,082
Urban	0,104	0,025	0,009	0,165	0,040	0,015	0,199	0,055	0,022
Grimm-Günther									
Total	0,555	0,209	0,100	0,618	0,229	0,110	0,472	0,160	0,073
Rural	0,634	0,241	0,117	0,687	0,258	0,125	0,533	0,183	0,083
Urban	0,147	0,039	0,015	0,273	0,083	0,035	0,203	0,057	0,023
Lachaud 2005									
Total	0,450	0,142	0,061	0,550	0,188	0,086	0,464	0,156	0,071
Rural	0,516	0,164	0,071	0,613	0,213	0,098	0,523	0,179	0,082
Urban	0,106	0,026	0,001	0,234	0,062	0,025	0,199	0,055	0,022

Source: Lachaud 2005

A major debate relates to the extent to which these various monetary calculations are supported by non-monetary measures of poverty. Both Grimm and Günther as well as Lachaud claim that non-monetary measures support their various standpoints. While Grimm and Günther refer in a general way to isolated social indicators, such as school enrolment rates, electricity connection, access to clean water and others, Lachaud provides a more detailed and thorough investigation of an ensemble of physical, human and social assets and their correlation with monetary measures of poverty. Further, he tests these correlations through multivariate regressions, and can in that way provide the stronger arguments. The result of his study is that in non-monetary terms, poverty incidence has increased somewhat over the total period 1994-2003. The factor driving this increase is decreasing social capital, he argues. Social capital is in his study measured through the proxy variable "flows of remittances". These fell, essentially because of the political crisis in neighbouring Côte d'Ivoire and the related expulsion of Burkinabé citizens. However, a weakness in Lachaud's proxy variable is that it is in fact a monetary factor, whereas the very idea was to introduce non-monetary variables in order to make for a robust test of the various estimates of the incidence of poverty. It would then be better to exclude this variable. If this factor is indeed disregarded, it turns out that non-monetary poverty remained fairly stable over the period, in terms of incidence, depth and inequality (Lachaud 2005:21ff).

We note from this discussion that relatively minor changes in the assumptions underlying the use of data have substantial effects on the poverty estimates obtained. Without passing final judgment on the credibility of available data, and on what estimate is more correct than the other, one may on balance conclude that poverty has remained rather stable over the whole period, with the exception of a probable peak in 1998. If there is any tendency for change, it would rather be that poverty may have increased somewhat, rather than decreased. Noteworthy of the calculations of Grimm and Günter is that while they find a decrease in poverty over the whole period, they simultaneously find a substantially higher level of poverty incidence as compared to the estimates of Lachaud and INSD.

In order to learn about the dynamics of poverty in Burkina Faso during these years, it is obvious that a closer look is necessary. In looking at disaggregated data, one aspect is that urban poverty has increased over the period. All sources are in agreement that the share of poor people living in urban areas increased between the two surveys of 1994 and 1998 – from 4.1 to 6.7 percent of all poor people in the country, or from 10 to more than 20 percent of all urban citizens. Figures for 2003 are more contested. [10] Only the INSD reports a constant increase in urban poverty, whereas both Grimm-Günter and Lachaud indicate a decrease from the 1998 peak. However, there is unanimous agreement that urban poverty in 2003 was substantially higher than it was in 1994, involving twice as many of the urban population, according to INSD.[11] This might, as already noted, be seen as somewhat contradictory, given that economic growth was faster in the service sector (5.6 percent annual average), followed by manufacturing (3.0 percent) and then agriculture (2.7 percent). Growth in the agricultural sector barely kept pace with population growth during the period 1996-2006 (World Bank 2007).

A closer study also indicates that poverty underwent rapid changes during these years, even if the net poverty rates seem to have remained fairly stable. Such changes were noticeable even over the short period between 1994-95 and 1998. Among the total number of poor, the share of people living in enduring poverty increased from 52 to almost 58 percent (54 to 59 percent in rural areas), between these years. Simultaneously, the share of people living in less severe poverty decreased. While some managed to move out of poverty, others fell more deeply into it. By introducing the concept of vulnerability, even more of the dynamics that occurred may be uncovered. Lachaud (2002) defines households with a 40 percent or greater chance of falling into poverty, or staying in poverty if already poor, as being vulnerable to poverty. This is obviously an arbitrary definition. However, it was chosen because median household vulnerability came very close to this level. The vulnerabilities of households were estimated by the use of a multinomial logistic method, where the estimate built on specific characteristics of the households.[12]

Overall, 51.4 percent of all the households in Burkina Faso were classified as vulnerable to poverty in 1998, according to threshold of a 40-percent risk of falling into poverty.[13] Even though the share of vulnerability was higher among those already experiencing poverty (69.5 percent of poor households were vulnerable to poverty), vulnerability was also prevalent among the non-poor. The share of non-poor households classified as vulnerable increased between the two surveys from 34.6 percent of the non-poor to 41.9 percent of the non-poor. What was more troublesome was that the level of vulnerability had increased significantly from 1994, both among those who already experienced poverty and among those who

---

10. Based on the estimates of Lachaud, urban poverty as a share of national poverty can be calculated to have decreased to some 3.5 percent: urban poverty rate of 19.9 percent times urbanisation rate of 17.8 percent. Sources: Ministry of the Economy and Finance, 2007: *Progress Report on the Implementation of the PRSP for Year 2006*, Ouagadougou, Burkina Faso; UN DESA, 2004: *World Urbanization Prospects, The 2003 revision, Data Tables and Highlights*, Population Division, New York.

11. See as well Bourdet and Thiombiano 2009:12ff.

12. Lachaud 2002:23 f. The household characteristics found to be relevant included demographic factors, education, migration and employment of household head, remittances, the number of household members and geographic location.

13. Lachaud 2002:8, table 1, column 5. Please note the miscalculation in the summaries for 1998, correct share is given here. In his text, Lachaud provides other shares, since he differentiates between vulnerable households depending on their expected level of consumption as well. This distinction is not considered here, since it does not add meaningful information, and in addition makes comparisons with other countries more difficult.

did not. To illustrate this in figures, one may refer to an increase in the national average level of vulnerability to poverty that households experienced: in 1994 this level was 37.9 percent, whereas in 1998 it had increased to 40.6 percent (Lachaud 2005:239).

POVERTY AMONG GROUPS WITH DIFFERENT LEVELS OF VULNERABILITY IN BURKINA FASO 1994 AND 1998.

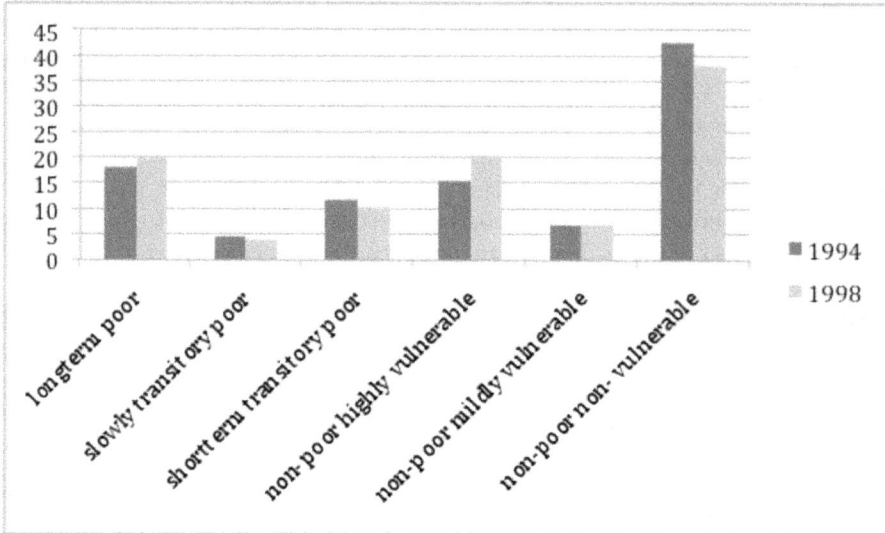

Source: Lachaud 2002

Both the group of long-term poor and of the highly vulnerable among the non-poor increased, whereas all the others decreased.

This pattern of deepening poverty, combined with increasing vulnerability among the non-poor was most accentuated in the smaller urban areas. In urban areas, the share of poor people that experienced enduring poverty had increased from 14 to 40 percent, while the non-poor experiencing vulnerability to poverty had increased from 5 to 18 percent as a share of all the non-poor. All other groups had become smaller. This happened despite the fact that poverty distribution had increased less in the two big cities, Ouagadougou and Bobo-Dioulasso (Lachaud 2003:234). Poverty in urban areas increased faster than the rate of urbanisation. In provincial cities, the increase in poverty rates was as much as 14 percent faster than the rate of urbanisation. According to Lachaud's analysis, it was the difficulty in accessing the labour market in combination with a decrease in social capital that was instrumental in this increasing poverty. Two categories of households were particularly hit by poverty: those headed either by informally employed or non-protected workers, or by the unemployed (ibid.:235).

There was also a particular gender aspect to urban poverty. In the national average, households headed by women were relatively less often poor than households headed by men. This difference became even more accentuated between 1994 and 1998, since poverty decreased in female-led households, while it increased in male-led households. But in urban areas, such differences did not exist. In the cities, poverty was instead equally distributed between male- and female-headed households (ibid.). Hence, the share of female-headed households experiencing poverty was relatively higher in urban than in rural areas.

Changing patterns of poverty may also be observed in rural areas, but to uncover these patterns may be a fairly intriguing undertaking. Starting with a description of the overall distribution of rural poverty, one has to note that the regions with the highest levels of poverty are spread throughout the country. They lie in the north, bordering Mali (North region, Boucle de Mouhoun), in the southwest, bordering Ghana and Côte d'Ivoire (South-West region), as well as in the central part of the country (South-Central region, Central Plateau and Centre-East region) (Bourdet and Thiombiano 2009). The regions with lower levels of poverty are also spread throughout the country. It is thus difficult to discern any clear geographical pattern to poverty. Furthermore, it is not obvious that any clear relationship exists between regional poverty and the economic activities most prevalent in any region (ibid.:19f).

However, when observing not the levels of poverty but the *change* in poverty levels during the 1994-98 and 1998-2003, it is possible to discern some interesting patterns. During the first sub-period, 1994-98, poverty remained relatively stable in the West, South-West and North-West regions, and at a lower level than the national average. In these regions, commercial agriculture and the growing of cash crops dominate, since natural conditions for agriculture are comparatively good in these areas. In the Centre, Centre-North and Centre-East regions, increased inequality was noted, with deepening poverty occurring at the same time as some people were experiencing material improvements. In these regions, subsistence farming and cattle raising predominates. In a third group of regions, North, Sahel, East and Centre-West, overall poverty decreased during 1994-98. Cattle-raising has a stronger standing in these regions, even if subsistence farming still predominates (Lachaud 2003:13, 233). A conclusion that can be drawn from changing poverty patterns within and between provinces is that reductions in the total share of poverty during this sub-period stemmed from falling levels of poverty in only four provinces, North, Sahel, East and Centre-West, together with migration (ibid:234).

In observing the second sub-period, 1998-2003, decreases in poverty were on average greatest in those regions that had a lower incidence of poverty. The North-Centre, Sahel, East and Centre-West regions displayed the biggest reductions in poverty, followed by the Centre-East region (Bourdet and Thiombiano 2009:49).

CHANGES IN POVERTY INCIDENCE PER REGION IN BURKINA FASO, 1994-2003

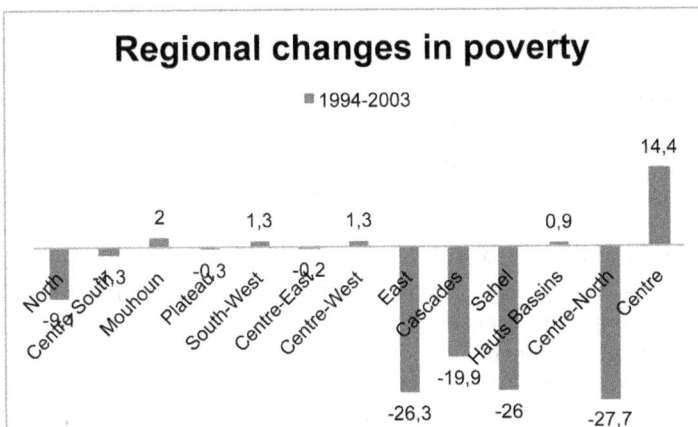

Source: INSD, Enquêtes priortaires I, II, III as recalculated in Grimm and Günther 2004:79.

What complicates the analysis is that dominant economic activities only partly follow regional boundaries. Furthermore, the changes that took place over the full period may not capture the dynamics that occurred during particular sub-periods. This is why the discussion above has been disaggregated into two sub-periods. We have, as well, tried to capture economic dynamics in a wider sense than just building on static regional specificities. This analysis was based on fieldwork conducted in Burkina Faso in the period 1999-2003, during which the author lived in the country for two full years and made several further visits to the country.

What most clearly distinguished two (Sahel and East) of the four regions where poverty decreased most in 1994-98 from other regions was the expansion of cattle raising that took place there. In a third of the four regions (North), the main characteristic was expansion in the growing of vegetables, while in the fourth (Centre-West) cotton growing expanded during this period. During the second period, 1998-2003, the most rapid reductions in poverty occurred in regions where cattle raising continued to expand in full or in part (Centre-North, Sahel, East, Centre-East). Somewhat slower reductions in poverty occurred in those regions where cotton growing expanded most (Centre-West, Cascades and Haut Bassins). Expansion in vegetable cultivation may also have had some poverty-reducing effects in the North region (Hårsmar 2004). Furthermore, whereas cotton growing does not seem to have led to poverty reduction over the whole period, 1994-2003, it might well have done so during the second sub-period, when more rapid expansion of cotton growing took place and, in particular, affected certain regions (Centre-West, Cascades, Haut Bassins).

In an earlier analysis (Hårsmar 2004), we found the cultivation of cotton and vegetables and cattle raising to be the three areas of greatest economic dynamism in the rural areas of Burkina Faso. What emerges from our current analysis is that the single most pronounced factor behind the reduction in poverty during 1994-2003 period appears to have been the expansion of cattle raising, followed by the growing of cotton and vegetables respectively. All these economic activities have their special particularities, which form the framework for their current and further expansion. We will look more closely at the preconditions under which cattle raising is expanding and contributing to poverty reduction.

Cattle raising and poverty reduction

Since the devaluation of the CFA franc in 1994, exports of cattle and meat from Burkina Faso have increased rapidly. Simultaneously, the domestic cattle and meat markets have developed as well, and average sizes of herds have increased. In the regions where cattle raising dominate, there has also been a shift in breeding practices. In the customary system, people belonging to the Peuhl ethnicity were the cattle raisers, with people from the Mossi ethnicity the sedentary cultivators. Mossis used to let their cattle out to the Peuhl, through a system of specialisation. However, increasing integration of cattle raising and crop farming has taken place. This inter-culture leads to improved soils, and enables technological evolution in agriculture. As part of the shifting practices, Mossis have gradually increased their own cattle breeding and raising, implying that they rent their cattle out to the Peuhl to a much lesser extent. The shift has been accompanied by decreasing levels of trust and increasing levels of conflict between Peuhl and Mossi (Hårsmar 2004:176ff).

It is not evident what long-term consequences these changes might bring. Seen broadly, the increased integration of cattle breeding and crop cultivation may either result in intensification – increased capital and labour investments per area – or in expansion – using lands not hitherto cultivated. The latter might also imply extensification (decreasing input of capital and labour per area) (Oksen 2001:304ff). One important factor influencing which of these paths will dominate is the extent to which conflicts between Peuhl and Mossi, between pastoralist cattlekeepers and sedentary farmers, will evolve over time. Decreasing trust between the groups has been evident as part of the pattern of changing practices. However, there are underlying factors that may explain these changes. Since the 1960s, rainfall has steadily decreased and become more erratic in cattle raising areas. The tree coverage has decreased, with attendant loss of biodiversity and soil degradation. It is underlying factors like this that have encouraged increased integration of cattle raising and crop cultivation. Despite the economic progress that has characterised cattle raising in Burkina Faso since the 1990s, the long-term effects remain unclear. This uncertainty will become more pronounced with the possible increase in average temperatures due to continued climatic change (Hårsmar 2004).

For the Mossi and the Peuhl that live in provinces in the North, Sahel, East and Centre-West regions, decreases in poverty levels thanks to the performance of cattle markets may very well coincide with increased levels of vulnerability, not only in the short term, but also over longer periods. It remains to be seen whether the overall effect of increased integration of cattle raising and crop cultivation will be improved intensification (with soil recovery) or increased extensification:

> Because animal husbandry is based on the interaction of two distinct socioeconomic and cultural groups each with their own land use system, expansion in one system leads to marginalization in the other. In contrast to dominant theories of agricultural intensification, the case points to the need to distinguish between agricultural expansion and intensification at least in situations of interrelated but distinct land use systems. (Oksen 2001:328)

Another factor that conditions the poverty-reducing effects of expanding markets in cattle is the evolution of inter-household relations, particularly in the Mossi group. Young men and women are the more dynamic economic categories. Young men involve themselves more than others in market-oriented cattle raising, whereas women raise smaller animals. For these activities to expand in the longer term, changes in traditional household structures seem inevitable (Hårsmar 2004:184).

In sum, we have generated a working hypothesis that the evolution of the cattle market has been the most important factor behind the overall change in poverty levels in Burkina Faso in recent years. This evolution is in evident in two larger trends – the increased demand for meat and meat products, particularly in neighbouring countries and from urban areas, and the gradually decreasing nutrient level of soils. Soil depletion calls for increased manuring for continued crop cultivation, which in turn calls for increased cattle holding by crop cultivators. The changes in the patterns of cattle keeping and crop cultivation, with sharply increased integration between the two, supports this interpretation. Increased economic growth, but in combination with changing cultural patterns, seems to be behind the poverty reduction in cattle raising groups and regions.

Increased poverty and crop cultivation

If changing practices in cattle keeping to some extent explain the decrease in poverty, what would explain the increases in observed poverty? The climb in urban poverty may be understood in terms of the problems in accessing the labour market, as argued by Lachaud. With urbanisation, the numbers of unemployed and salaried workers without social protection have increased. It is in these two groups that vulnerability is highest in urban areas (Lachaud 2002:14). The interpretation Lachaud provides is that labour markets are malfunctioning, particularly in light of high entry barriers. Urban poverty has been increasing most in smaller and medium sized urban areas.

But what is the possible background to the increased incidence of enduring poverty primarily in rural areas? Here, we have to look particularly at households that concentrate on growing staple crops in the Plateau, Centre, Centre-South, South-West and Centre-East sub-regions. Most of these regions constitute the central part of the Mossi Plateau, where subsistence agriculture dominates (Lachaud 2003:235f). Bourdet and Thiombiano (2009:21) indicate that the share of subsistence is indeed positively correlated with the incidence of poverty as measured at the level of the regions.

In a previous work, we explained the comparatively low level of economic diversification on the Mossi Plateau by referring to the particular pattern of indigenous institutions that characterise Mossi society (Hårsmar 2004). A set of institutions upholding a) social relations; b) the household as the primary production unit; c) customary land tenure; and d) the adherence to local power structures together create a web that results in change inertia among cultivators. This inertia translates into foregone economic opportunities. As long as the forces that keep the above institutional web together are stronger than concurrent dis-integrating relationships, poverty will prevail, and possibly deepen. As a complementary factor, the deepening of poverty can also be understood as a consequence of long-term soil degradation and worsening conditions for cultivation (ibid.: chaps 4 and 5). Distance to market or other expressions of market connectivity, however, do not explain the prevalence of poverty in the areas under study. Regions and areas where poverty has decreased are as disconnected from markets as these regions are. If anything, the whole of Burkina Faso could be described as having low market connectivity, since the costs of transportation and trade are higher for Burkina Faso than for other countries in West Africa (Bourdet and Thiombiano 2009:36). For instance, it is three times more expensive to import a container to Burkina Faso than to Benin, Togo or Nigeria, and seven times more expensive than to import a container to China.

There are, even in the areas where enduring poverty has increased, opportunities for improved economic activities and growth, primarily in the form of the cultivation and marketing of cotton and vegetables. These practices are, however, mainly practised as side activities, often undertaken by household members with a somewhat freer role (primarily youth and women), but who are hindered in undertaking them as full time activities.

In sum, the economic activities that need to be analysed and understood in relation to poverty patterns in Burkina Faso are dynamic ones, such as cattle raising, cotton and vegetable cultivation, as well as the basic activity of growing staples, which is rather more connected to stagnation and stable or increasing poverty. The agricultural sector, despite efforts at economic diversification, continues to be essential.

2.5 Tanzania

Tanzania shares many important characteristics with Burkina Faso. The dominant economic sector is agriculture, and within this sector smallholders predominate. About 80 percent of the population earns its living from agriculture, and cultivated plots regularly amount to between one and three hectares per smallholder household. Staple food crops, such as maize, rice, millet and sorghum, wheat, cassava and beans, account for some 85 percent of production, whereas export crops account for about 12 percent. Much of the cultivation is for subsistence, but agriculture still accounts for some 45 percent of GDP.

Poverty is widespread. In 1991-92, 38.6 percent of the population was living below the poverty line.[14] In 2000-01, this share had decreased somewhat to 35.7 percent. The share is still decreasing, but the release of the figure from the 2007 survey, showing that 33.3 percent were still living below the poverty line, caused some debate. Poverty reduction was seen to have been all too slow, given that GDP had grown by an annual average of about 7 percent since 2001. Population growth has over the same period averaged about 2.1 percent annually (US Census Bureau 2009).

Over the full period from 1991-92 to 2007, there has been a decline in poverty of about five percentage points. There has simultaneously been a small decline in the poverty gap, which measures the depth of poverty and which implies the distance between the poverty line and the average position of those living under this line. In spite of this, the absolute number of poor people has increased, and amounted to 12.9 million in 2007. The decline in poverty share has been largest in the capital Dar es Salaam, and least in the rural areas. Poverty remains an overwhelmingly rural phenomenon, and about 83 percent of the poor live in rural areas. In 2001-02 this share was even higher, 88 percent, which reflects the fast rate of urbanisation taking place. Another tendency is that inequality has risen somewhat over the full period. The greatest increases in inequality have taken place in Dar es Salaam, whereas inequality has remained more or less stable in rural areas.

The data on household expenditure show that national average real consumption has increased by some 5 percent between 2000-01 and 2007. Furthermore, they indicate that shares of purchased food have fallen as part of overall consumption in both urban and rural areas, as have medical and educational expenditures. This is something that would be expected when real incomes rise. However, it might also reflect increases in non-food prices.

Studies of vulnerability that cover the whole of Tanzania do not, to our knowledge, exist. However, in 2006 Sarris and Karfakis studied the level of vulnerability in two regions, Kilimanjaro and Ruvuma. This study was later included in a more extensive volume, edited by Christaensen and Sarris (2007). The Kilimanjaro region, located in the north, bordering Kenya, is the richer and more economically diversified region of the two. The Ruvuma region is located in the south, bordering Mozambique, and households there are generally more oriented towards subsistence farming. Average consumption per capita is 20 percent lower in Ruvama than in Kilimanjaro. The total value of productive assets, including land, livestock and production equipment, is more than twice as high in Kilimanjaro as in Ruvuma (Christiaensen and Sarris 2007:13f).

The households included in the two surveyed regions were exclusively rural. The shocks that rural households in these two regions face were placed in four categories: a) climatic and agricultural; b) health, including death and illness of household members; c) economic, including unemployment and negative price shocks; and d) asset shocks, including loss of

---

14. The Tanzanian Household budget surveys operate with two distinct poverty levels: a food poverty line, calculated as the cost of meeting the minimum adult calorific requirement with a food consumption pattern typical of the poorest 50 percent of the population; and a basic needs poverty line, which adds to the food poverty line the costs of the non-food expenditures that the poorest 25 percent of the population bears (HBS 2007). Here we refer to the basic needs poverty line.

livestock, theft, eviction, fire. The threshold level for vulnerability applied was the same as in the Burkina Faso study, 0.4, implying that households facing a risk of 40 percent or higher of becoming poor in the next period were classified as vulnerable. Differences between the two regions were substantial. In Kilimanjaro, 22 percent of all households were vulnerable (9.7 percent of the non-poor and 48 percent of the poor run this risk). In Ruvuma, 70 percent were vulnerable (49 percent of the non-poor and 87 percent of the poor run this risk). It is worth noting that if the threshold of vulnerability is increased to 0.5 or 0.6, the share of the vulnerable in each group decreases by only a few percentage points. Hence, it seems that the groups of vulnerable households are fairly stable (Sarris and Karfakis 2006).

In Kilimanjaro, coffee is the dominant cash crop. However, since world market prices for coffee have been declining, particularly since the late 1990s, many farmers have diversified into other crops or gone into wage labour. Bananas sold to Dar es Salaam have been an alternative cash crop for the former coffee growers of Kilimanjaro. However, it is not the case that coffee growing as such provides a better living than growing other cash crops or engaging in other economic activities. For instance, the two districts within Kilimanjaro that have the biggest share of coffee growers (Rombo, where 83 percent grow coffee, and Hai, with 79 percent growing coffee) have respectively the highest (56.2 percent in Rombo) and lowest (24.5 percent in Hai) incidence of poverty of the five districts in Kilimanjaro (ibid.:12). Obviously, the picture is more complex.

In Ruvuma, cash crop production follows geographical as well as ethnic lines. The Matengo people in Mbinga district primarily produce coffee; the Ngoni people in Namtumbo district mainly produce tobacco; whereas the Yao people in Tunduru district grow cashew nuts. The incidence of poverty is lower in the coffee growing district (56 percent), higher in the tobacco growing district (70 percent), and even more pronounced in the cashew growing district (77 percent) (ibid.).

Interesting demographic differences between the two regions can be found. Household heads are on average ten years older in Kilimanjaro, 53.5 versus 43.4 years. Dependency ratios, as well as the share of female-headed households, are higher in Kilimanjaro.[15] In addition, the average age of the population is higher in Kilimanjaro. Hoffmann et al. interpret this as the result of outmigration, a finding also supported by the fact that 26 percent of households in Kilimanjaro receive remittances, against 13 percent in Ruvuma. There is a substantially higher pressure on lands in Kilimanjaro than in Ruvuma. Practically all lands in Kilimanjaro are cultivated, and the cost of land is much higher than in Ruvuma. This might be a push factor behind migration. At the same time, it strongly contributes to the higher value of assets held in Kilimanjaro. The larger herds of livestock are another important factor behind the higher value of assets in this region. Moreover, Hoffmann et al. also point to the importance of infrastructure for economic progress. Connectivity in terms of paved roads and a widespread GSM phone system gives Kilimanjaro region greater opportunities than the Ruvuma region.

With these differences as background, one may note that when coffee prices declined on the world market after 2000, cultivators in Kilimanjaro continued their long-term shift away from coffee, while cultivators in Ruvuma planted more coffee trees. Bananas became a replacement cash crop in Kilimanjaro, as did economic activities other than crop cultivation. It

---

15. The average dependency ratio is 51 percent in Kilimanjaro, as against 48 percent in Ruvuma. The share of female-headed households is 12.5 percent, as against 7.7 (Christaensen and Sarris 2007: Tables 2.3 and 2.4).

is, however, important to underscore a nuance here. While rural households in Kilimanjaro diversified into a larger number of economic activities, the concentration of value held in particular assets was higher than it was for average households in Ruvuma. This is measured by an index called the Herfindahl index.

Such differences between Ruvuma and Kilimanjaro tend to outweigh similarities in social capital and in organisational levels between the two regions. The incidence of poverty in both Kilimanjaro and Ruvuma was substantially higher than the national averages established in the national household budget surveys a few years earlier. In Kilimanjaro, around 40 percent of all households were poor, and in Ruvuma around 63 percent were. However, since poverty is primarily a rural phenomenon, and all households in the Ruvuma and Kilimanjaro surveys were rural, higher levels of poverty are to be expected. What is more interesting is the comparison between groups who were poor in 2003 and in 2004 respectively. In Kilimanjaro, 16 percent of all households fell into poverty, whereas slightly less than 18 percent moved out of poverty during these two years. That left 66 percent of households that stayed in the same category between these two years. In Ruvuma, 68 percent of households stayed in the same categories (poor or non-poor), whereas 15.5 percent moved out of poverty and 16 percent fell into it between these two years. The fact that movements into and out of poverty were so similar in size thus hides the large transitory character of poverty in both these regions. Household budget surveys providing net measures of poverty cannot capture these large movements over the years.

Shocks of various kinds hit poor and non-poor in Ruvuma and Kilimanjaro in a fairly similar pattern. Shocks may be climatic, agriculture-oriented, health-related, economic or asset-related. Some of the shocks hit the whole population simultaneously, while other shocks struck differently from individual to individual. The shocks might have been creeping, or appeared without prior notice. Over the five year period 1999-2003, about two-thirds of households in both regions reported at least one livelihood shock. Most households faced more than one shock. The most common shock was death and illness. Drought was the second most common type of shock in Kilimanjaro, but uncommon in Ruvuma, since rain patterns are steadier there. Price shocks were not common, despite the fact that prices of some important crops had been falling. However, these changes were more of a long-term character and hence not experienced as shocks to the same extent.

Almost three-quarters of the households who faced shocks used their savings or sold assets to cope. The second most important strategy was to secure assistance from others – family, friends or various organisations. About 30 percent of the affected tried to earn additional income, and almost as many lowered or changed their food and other consumption patterns. A very small group was forced to sell productive assets, or leave their homes. Overall, it seemed households in the two regions were quite able to deal with the shocks without too seriously compromising future earnings or falling into poverty. There were, of course, differences, with poor households receiving slightly less aid from others and having to change their food consumption habits more often than others. But the larger picture is one of a fairly even pattern of coping with shocks. An important exception was that households facing exceptional shocks (i.e., a shock hitting individually) received almost twice as much aid from others as those hit by shocks facing everyone simultaneously. In addition, additional income was not generated as much in cases of exceptional as in cases of covariate shock.

Even if shocks hit the two regions in a similar pattern, vulnerability to poverty differs between the regions. Overall vulnerability is significantly higher in Ruvuma, as stated above. In both regions, the levels of vulnerability are higher among the poor than the non-poor. Beyond this, it is contextual factors that determine vulnerability in the two regions. In Kilimanjaro, net food buyers are more vulnerable than net food sellers, whereas the opposite is true in Ruvuma. In Ruvuma, vulnerability is highest among cashew nut growers, whereas no difference can be noted among growers of various cash crops in Kilimanjaro.

Kilimanjaro region

Larsson (2001) describes a gradual long-term adjustment taking place on the slopes of Mount Meru during the whole colonial and postcolonial period: "Our historical review suggests that family farming on Mount Meru has been extremely adaptive to external conditions since the onset of colonial rule" (Larsson 2001: 440). Mount Meru is situated in the Arusha region, and is thus not part of the Kilimanjaro region. However, it borders the Moshi urban and Hai districts in the Kilimanjaro region, and displays a similar economic structure to these districts. Hence, information on livelihoods on the slopes of Mount Meru has relevance for the situation in Kilimanjaro region as well. The long-term shift in Mount Meru was triggered by an increasing scarcity of land due to population growth, but was also fuelled by changes in preferences and cultural practices. In particular, the younger inhabitants have to an increasing degree ceased to see subsistence agriculture as a viable livelihood strategy. Off-farm economic activities and migration have become an increasingly important part of livelihood strategies. In particular, liberalisation has opened up new opportunities, while at the same time leading to increased costs and increased commercialisation of rural areas. However, rather than discussing a process of de-peasantisation, Larsson talks of the increasing practice of part-time farming, in his terms, an "agricultural adjustment". Even while earning more and more of their income from sources other than agriculture, peasants retain their farms and keep up their cultivation. The peasant identity is strong, and continued access to land, even small plots, is important to people's identity: "Tradition, however, has no doubt contributed to the preservation of family farming and prevented the emergence of a landless class of former peasants" (ibid.:450).

While retaining their land, peasants have increasingly cultivated a larger number of cash crops, as well as venturing into cattle raising. The changes have to a large degree benefited from advice and other input from outsiders (ibid.:432). Larsson's empirical studies further show that both the on- and off-farm diversification that household heads have undertaken has had a positive impact on farm output and productivity, for instance through investments in improved soil fertility (ibid.:292ff). The flexibility that over the past decade or so has allowed poverty levels to decrease and well-being to increase among peasants in the Kilimanjaro province can, according to Larsson, be ascribed to this longer term shift in habits and livelihoods. It is increasing population pressure and a subsequent intensification of agriculture that have increased the spread of markets and infrastructure, and hence increased prosperity. However, the thesis that commercialisation as such has driven the change cannot be supported, he argues (ibid.:443f).

Ruvuma region

Changes taking place over the last 25 years in the Songea rural district in Ruvuma region have been studied by Ponte (2002). Songea used to be one of the major food-producing districts in Tanzania, due to national policies of pan-territorial pricing, fertiliser subsidies, national projects and government purchases. However, with the abolition of pan-territorial pricing from 1982 onward, this situation changed. The unfavourable location in relation to major markets made this district uncompetitive, especially as the transport infrastructure was bad or nonexistent. The further liberalisation of food crop markets and, in the mid-1990s, eventually of export crop markets, placed this district in an even less favourable position (Ponte 2002:99f). Attempts at shifting into export markets such as neighbouring Malawi or Zambia met with administrative, political as well of economic difficulties (ibid.:105ff).

The overall outcome of the liberalising reforms affecting Songea rural district was, according to Ponte, increased commercialisation of rural life. This meant that more goods were available for sale, but also that price levels increased, as did the cost of living. Furthermore, there was a shift in cultivation practices among peasants from slow-growing to fast-growing crops. This was done to raise money more quickly, but also in order to avoid problems related to demands from extended family and neighbours on the crops produced. Crops that deteriorate more quickly cannot be stored for long and must be sold before anyone can come and ask for a share. Ponte also noted an overall decrease in total net farm income (ibid.:115f, 129). While there was increased participation in off-farm economic activities, economic diversification did not lead to increased levels of income in this region (ibid.:124-40). This is generally different from the effects of economic diversification in the Kilimanjaro region (Hoffman et al. 2007:21). Furthermore, the indications are that one group with a decreasing incidence of poverty in the Ruvuma region is the tobacco growers. While coffee and cashew nut producers in Ruvuma have in recent years increasingly concentrated their production on one cash crop – despite falling prices – tobacco growers have shown signs of shifting from dependency on a single cash crop. However, tobacco growers still earn higher shares of their total income from their main cash crop than the other two groups (ibid.:16, 25).

Ponte made his observations during the liberalisation period of the 1980s and 1990s. During these years, what initially kept peasants from shifting among crops were by-laws prescribing a minimum acreage to be cultivated with specified cash crops, as well as the fact that only one buyer existed – the cooperative union. When the by-laws were gradually relaxed and the monopoly of the cooperative abolished, peasants did in fact shift crops. In the new liberalised situation, difficulties in accessing inputs as well as accessing produce markets due to, for instance, high transport costs became new hindrances. This led to a situation in which a region whose production was once so important found itself increasingly marginalised.

2.6 Burkina Faso and Tanzania compared
Notes on the importance of agriculture

It is both difficult and potentially misleading to describe the essential differences and similarities in the poverty situation in Burkina Faso and Tanzania. In this study, we have treated the issues first at an aggregate level, then supplemented the description by reference to evolutions at the micro-level. Real understanding of why people are falling into, or moving out of poverty, demands deep contextual knowledge. However, consideration of the differences emerging from this aggregate-level discussion combined with micro-level studies allows for the formulation of tentative hypotheses for further testing.

One message that emerges from these two cases is that the kind of agricultural production undertaken to a large extent defines the opportunities for moving out of or falling into poverty. Agricultural production systems and rural livelihoods more broadly differ substantially between various regions in both these countries. Because of this, it is essential to study the regional variations of poverty dynamics. Furthermore, before comparing cases from the two countries, it is informative to reflect on what it means to be dependent on agriculture to the extent that people are in Burkina Faso and Tanzania. What we have been discussing above are economic activities essentially related to agriculture and other natural resources. Since the use of land is central to economic activities, geography and agroclimatic conditions will be essential to the economic outcome as well as for the depth and incidence of poverty. Soil nutrients, rainfall patterns and a number of ecosystem services have to be taken into consideration in the analysis of poverty. They are the underlying, long term-factors influencing the livelihoods of people.

Since agriculture plays such an important economic role in these two countries, as well as in other SSA countries, a wider underlying issue is what the economic possibilities are for broad-based agricultural development. Many arguments have been put forward over time. For instance, the thesis of increased commercialisation leading to "de-peasantisation" (Bryceson et al. 2000) has been set against the arguments about a number of economic, political and institutional factors at regional, national and international levels that limit the options for small-scale farming (Djurfelt et al. 2005:132). The aim of this study is not to join that discussion, but rather to dwell on narrower reasons certain groups of people fare ill in terms of poverty.

As background to this discussion, it is important to note that since people's relationships to land play important roles for identity, there will be multiple overlaps between what may be interpreted as religious or cultural aspects of land use and economic aspects. Indigenous institutions will be important, and these are probably not primarily structured to fulfil economic functions. It is important to understand the roles and functions of these institutions in order to understand economic behaviour in relation to natural resource management. There are reasons such institutions may be particularly central in African agriculture: weak state capacity implies that activities which in other places are regulated by law remain informal and social in character in rural Africa. Secondly, weak infrastructure and low population density probably makes social norms more resilient in the face of changes in the economic environment.

Another message that emerges from the study is that institutional arrangements play a central role in defining the limits of economic expansion in the different agricultural activities. Generally, agriculture is an economic sector with high levels of risk and uncertainty. These stem from, among others, climatic and natural conditions, from badly functioning markets and underdeveloped infrastructure, from dependence on volatile world markets. Risk-sharing and consumption-smoothing practices become central, including the role of credit and insurance. In areas characterised by high risk, it is often observed that informal institutions play major roles, particularly in areas where poverty is widespread and economic opportunities are few (De Laiglesia 2006:54ff).

There is an extensive literature on the role of institutions in agricultural development in SSA. Dorward and Kydd (2004), for instance, argue that the absence of local markets and market institutions is a critical constraint on livelihood changes and economic growth. Because so many elements are lacking at the same time, there are "coordination risks" – most actors are unwilling to invest since their investments would be profitable only if others invest at the same time. There are also "risks of opportunism", since certain actors in the supply chain might be able to use monopoly or monopsony positions to exploit others. Such risks may result in at least some of the simultaneously needed investments not being made (Dorward et al. 2006).

However, what we have observed in this study is cases where indigenous institutions have operated for a long time and where they remain functional even when new market opportunities open up. Even if Dorward and Kydd's coordination and opportunism risks can be overcome and new market opportunities can emerge, the shift from indigenous to more purely market-supportive institutions takes a long time, and our knowledge of the dynamics of this process is still limited.

Based on other studies, it has been argued that indigenous institutions may contribute to the lack of economic progress and the lack of poverty reduction principally for three reasons (De Laiglesia 2006; Elbers et al. 2007, 2009):

- Risk reduction may imply sub-optimal allocation of resources, especially egalitarian norms that can also "tax" efforts at accumulation in a growth-reducing way;
- Indigenous institutions are costly to uphold, hence resources that could be put to productive use are allocated to other purposes;
- Institutions and norms may be exclusionary, for instance of women, strangers and others. This implies that not all the available productive capacity will be used for productive purposes.

Furthermore, institutions may be instrumental in causing inequality. Tilly (2008) discusses two general mechanisms through which this can happen – "exploitation" and "opportunity hoarding". Exploitation implies that someone first enlists the efforts of others in the production of value through a certain resource, only to exclude them from benefiting from the full value of their efforts. Even though this may occur, this is not the most significant way in which institutions contribute to inequality. More relevant is opportunity hoarding, which implies that control of a resource that produces value is limited to an in-group. And, as we have just noted, informal institutions often exclude subcategories: other ethnic groups, immigrants, women, etc.

Another, more subtle effect is that social norms concerning the division of labour are upheld, as are those norms concerning what economic activities certain social groups may undertake. The issue of group identity may be strong in this respect as the application of such norms has the effect of raising very high barriers for outsiders wanting to enter possibly profitable economic activities. This might happen when an in-group controls production factors such as land, other natural resources or animals that they have the power to allocate or lend to others. Besides this, religious or semi-religious beliefs or taboos are often connected with certain activities. For instance, blacksmithing is connected with a great number of taboos in Burkinabé society. The result is that this particular activity has been the privilege of a particular ethnic group.

The importance of indigenous institutions in dealing with risk and in affecting economic growth negatively is highlighted in a vast and quickly growing literature.[16] To move further on these issues, detailed studies of institutional arrangements in the various regions become necessary.

Long-term changes, short-term impact

Another pattern that emerges from a comparison of these two countries is that those people who have been able to move out of poverty have, on the surface of it, capitalised on some economic upturn. Such upturns have either occurred in one particular activity or in

---

16. See, for instance, Elbers et al. 2007 and 2009.

one product, or more generally, come about by diversifying into more prosperous activities. However, sociological and anthropological studies indicate rather that there are longer-term processes underlying such changes. Despite the fact that some activities have brought increased prosperity, the dynamic activities seem to be constantly confined to certain geographically areas and/or ethnic groups. It is rare for people to change their core economic activities across geographic and ethnic boundaries, even if profits are higher elsewhere. This is particularly the case in Burkina Faso, where, for instance, the new form of cattle raising is limited to those provinces, regions and population groups that have been involved in such activities for a long time. Furthermore, in this case the indications are that it is not primarily new economic opportunities that drive the change, but rather longer-term challenges to livelihoods, such as decreasing soil fertility and increasing population pressure.

In those cases where people have managed to diversify into new economic areas, they have often fared better in terms of poverty levels. The question then arises, what keeps so many groups and people from diversifying into new economic activities? Before attempting an answer, however, this question needs to be refined. The concept of "diversification" is problematic in the sense that it can refer both to on-farm and off-farm diversification. Further, some off-farm activities generate increased levels of income and are a source of accumulation, whereas other off-farm activities generate very small incomes, and are undertaken as a risk-reducing survival strategy. The relevant question should be, what hinders peasants from undertaking economic diversification of the sort that leads to economic accumulation?

Answers to this question must, of course, be provided locally, in each context. Hårsmar (2004) dwelled on this, arguing that *change inertia* related to the upholding of an indigenous institutional web could explain the lack of economic diversification in Burkina Faso.[17] Generally, in that country the strength and persistence of indigenous institutions is more pronounced than in Tanzania. The latter has had a different history, with more government penetration of rural areas and rural life. Hence, in Tanzania a different story emerges. Ponte describes an evolution in the Ruvuma region where peasants are actively shifting to cash crops in order to meet the increasing commercialisation of rural life, as well as to avoid the difficulties of egalitarian norms and collective security systems. The top five cash crops cultivated and sold over a ten-year period remained almost the same in this region. However, their order of importance changed drastically, with those cash crops that require shorter periods of cultivation and that deteriorate quicker becoming the most frequently cultivated. A conclusion that can be drawn is that, in Ruvuma, indigenous institutions are not upheld to the same extent as they are in Burkina Faso. Such institutions are, rather, being eroded and seen as hindrances to the well-being of households. Customary social negotiations over access to land, labour, markets and other resources have increasingly been replaced by contractual relations. This is also part of what Ponte calls the "commercialisation of rural life" (Ponte 2002:121ff). From a situation where market institutions were initiated and run by government and cooperatives, more market-friendly institutions have emerged in Ruvuma,

---

17. Hårsmar (2004) argued that "resistance to change" was the important variable behind non- or insufficient diversification. However, this turned out to be an unfortunate misrepresentation, since the term could be interpreted as relating to the willingness of people to change. Hence, "change inertia" is a better term, since it is more neutral. This factor may also be interpreted as an indicator of the strength of prevailing indigenous institutions. Moreover, De Laiglesia (2006) has argued that informal institutions may to a large degree explain the growth or lack of growth in agriculture in SSA.

as they have in Tanzania in general. However, for a weakly connected region such as Ruvuma, the result seems to have been decreased market connection, eventually contributing to a rather stable production pattern in terms of what crops to cultivate, as mentioned above (Hoffman et al. 2007:16).

In the case of the high level of economic diversification that is taking place in the Kilimanjaro region, indications are that there has been a rather long-term process leading to the current situation, spanning many decades. Even in this area, which is better connected to markets, economic behaviour seems to have been guided by some kind of institutional structure that has evolved over an extended period.

In the areas where poverty is more widespread, both in Burkina Faso and in Tanzania, many groups continue to cultivate the cash crops they have traditionally cultivated. As we have seen, the reasons for this vary from one place to another. What in Burkina Faso can be described as change inertia is in Ruvuma, Tanzania a matter of lack of alternatives. Following Ponte's study, we can conclude that economic liberalisation reforms have had negative effects in terms of increasing poverty levels for groups in this region.

In the Kilimanjaro region of Tanzania, dependency on only one particular cash crop is low. When shocks happen, or other problems arise, people are in general able to shift from such dependency. This seems to be made possible by the relatively higher savings and assets, by higher inflows of remittances and by a greater connectivity to markets as compared with Ruvuma. People have more flexibility, and may therefore weather the storms better.

There are differences in poverty and vulnerability levels in the Kilimanjaro region, in particular between the Same and the Hai districts. These differences may relate to connectivity, since the Same district has less infrastructure and access to services (ibid.:18). In Ruvuma, dependency on single cash crops is much higher among farming households, savings and asset levels generally lower and poverty levels generally deeper.

Throughout all of the compared cases, market connectivity stands out as more important than other factors, at least in Tanzania. It is also important in Burkina Faso, but needs to be understood there in slightly different terms. Normally, connectivity relates to distance in combination with the availability of communications. Better roads and phone lines increase trade flows, particularly over shorter distances. But this is not necessarily all there is to connectivity. Cattle keepers in Burkina Faso do not generally have access to good roads, and their phone system is far from highly functional. Nevertheless, they manage to gain access to their markets mainly through a large cattle market in the city of Pouytenga in the eastern part of the country, to which the cattle can be walked. This might not work in future, since increasing competition will lead to an increased need for road transportation for animals.

In cases where market connectivity is low, and where alternative sources of finance such as remittances are low, we have noted high dependency on the cultivation of single cash crops. This might be due to change inertia or to the fact that not many other options exist. We have also traced the greater importance of indigenous institutions in such cases. It might be the case that indigenous institutions are more enduring and less poverty-reducing when connectivity to markets as well as the outside world is low. Alternatively, it might be that when market institutions are not functioning sufficiently well, people have no other system to rely on. De Laiglesia (2006:54ff) points to the fact that insufficient provision of infrastructure leads to increased transaction costs. This in turn would tend to suggest a situation in which indigenous institutions thrive because they provide alternative forms of insurance, credit, market information and other functions that are essential for economic activities when markets are absent or not functioning well.

But even in cases where market connectivity is much higher because the necessary infrastructure exists, the institutional pattern plays an important role. In the Kilimanjaro region, it was only after a long-term process of change, driven by increasing population pressure and land scarcity, that people have increasingly ventured into off-farm production of various kinds.

2.7 Conclusions

Studies relying on quantitative methods have shown that new patterns are emerging in poverty dynamics in Burkina Faso and Tanzania. Despite fairly rapid economic growth, poverty has remained stable or been reduced less than expected in both countries. Vulnerability to poverty has simultaneously increased over the last two decades. What we have also seen is that there are important regional differences in poverty dynamics. A central task of this study has been to analyse what the reasons for these differences are. By combining quantitative regional analysis with existing qualitative studies conducted in the same regions and concentrated on the same population groups, we have been able to reach a deeper understanding of the change processes under way in these two countries.

While overall levels of poverty incidence have fallen slightly, both Burkina Faso and Tanzania have witnessed an increase in the level of enduring poverty since the first half of the 1990s. The share of people caught in long-term poverty is increasing in areas where people generally are dependent on subsistence agriculture supplemented by some cash crop farming. One important factor that might explain the lack of poverty reduction in many regions is the low level of market connectivity. In regions where this is the case, change inertia or lack of viable economic options contribute to widespread and continuing use of indigenous institutions of kinds geared towards collective security rather than economic accumulation.

There are in these processes important differences between Burkina Faso and Tanzania. One is that the customary institutional web is stronger and more influential in Burkina Faso. In Tanzania, the history of deeper government and state penetration into rural areas implies that other types of institutions are more important in guiding market behaviour there. Again, differences in the level of market connectivity may be important. It is crucial to take such variation into consideration in analysing economies in distinct countries.

However, what we have seen in all the discussed cases in these two countries is that changes resulting in reduced poverty are *not primarily* driven by the emergence of new economic opportunities. More important is a long-term underlying process of changing rural livelihoods. A central finding is that changes in poverty in these two countries are primarily driven by regional differences in agriculturally based livelihoods. The particular agro-ecological and economic conditions that frame the changes in those livelihoods also set the framework for poverty reductions or increases.

In all these change processes, the institutional structure plays a central role. Norms and institutional webs continue to guide peasant behaviour in all the regional cases discussed. Processes of change are characterised by long-term factors, such as shifting agro-ecological conditions and increasing population pressure. Hence, the indications are that the impact of economic reforms and other political shifts is conditioned by both the institutional arrangements and such long-term changes.

It has as well been noted that increased vulnerability is emerging at the same time as the overall incidence of poverty is slowly decreasing. Poverty is affecting new groups of people, and in new patterns. Simultaneous movements in and out of poverty are quite substantial, as a result. When increasing numbers of people manage to move out of poverty, increasing numbers of people at the same time fall into it. Particularly in rural areas, climatic factors seem to be highly relevant to the level of vulnerability. More effort should be put into the study of climate and poverty.

Another component in the changing pattern of poverty is that the urbanisation of poverty is on the rise. In urban settings, the informal character of work and the subsequent difficulty in connecting informal and formal labour markets seem to be an important factor. This is an area that should attract increased attention, as the urbanisation rate is high and urban poverty is increasing.

Despite the fact that we initially chose to study Burkina Faso and Tanzania because of their many similarities, we have noted that there are also important differences between the two. The nature of the institutional web influencing economic behaviour is one difference. Where Burkina Faso is a society where customary patterns are still strong, Tanzania is somewhat more characterised by market-oriented institutions. The nature of market connectivity is also somewhat different between the countries. What may be concluded about the possibility of generalizing results to other countries in SSA is that context is important, and that not only country, but also regional and social group characteristics need to be taken into consideration in studies of poverty.

As an attempt to combine new methods from various disciplines, this study has, it is hoped, shown that new and deeper knowledge can be gained through such approaches. However, there are obvious limitations to what can be achieved by re-studying existing works. Collaboration between researchers from various disciplines in the design, fieldwork and analysis phases would provide more and deeper insights. For instance, primarily those traditions such as economic anthropology, economic sociology or geography would be able to contribute enormously to increased understanding by complementing what emerges from economic studies undertaken at a more aggregated level. The analysis could also be taken further by adding more traditional economic studies, such as tracing the important changes in relative prices and institutions affecting agricultural markets – for instance, inputs and markets for cattle, cotton and vegetables. More work remains to be done.

REFERENCES

Addison, T., D. Hulme and R. Kanbur, 2008: "Poverty Dynamics: Measurement and Understanding from an Interdisciplinary Perspective", BWPI Working Paper 19, University of Manchester.

Alkire, S. and J. Foster, 2008: "Counting and Multidimensional Poverty", Working Paper 7, Oxford Poverty and Human Development Initiative, Queen Elizabeth House, Oxford University.

Anderson, D. and V. Broch-Due, 1999: *The Poor are Not Us – Poverty and Pastoralism.* Oxford: James Currey; Nairobi: EAEP; and Athens: Ohio University Press.

Bardhan, P. and I. Ray, 2006: "Methodological Approaches in Economics and Anthropology", Q-Squared Working Paper 17, University of Toronto.

Berry, S., 1985: *Fathers Work for their Sons.* Berkeley: University of California Press.

–, 1993: *No Condition is Permanent.* Madison: University of Wisconsin Press.

Besley, T. and R. Burgess, 2002: "Redistribution, Growth and Poverty Reduction", LSE (mimeo) London.

Bourdet, Y. and T. Thiombiano, 2009: *Burkina Faso ou les infortunes de l'enclavement,* Country Economic Report 2009:1, Sida, Stockholm.

Bryceson, D., C. Kay and J. Mooij (eds), 2000: *Disappearing peasantries – Rural Labour in Latin America, Asia and Africa.* London: Intermediate Technology Publications.

Chambers, R., 2006: "What is Poverty? Who asks? Who answers? in *Poverty in Focus,* UNDP International Poverty Centre, December 2006.

Christiaensen, L. and A. Sarris, 2007: "Rural household vulnerability and insurance against commodity risks – Evidence from the United Republic of Tanzania", FAO, Trade and Markets Division, Rome.

Christiaensen, L., L. Demery and S. Paternostro, 2003: "Macro and Micro Perspectives of Growth and Poverty in Africa", *World Bank Economic Review* 17(3):317-47.

De Laiglesia, J.R. 2006: "Institutional Bottlenecks for Agricultural Development", Working Paper 248, OECD Development Centre, Paris.

Djurfeldt, G., H. Holmén, M. Jirström and R. Larsson, 2005: *The African Food Crisis – Lessons from the Asian Green Revolution.* Wallington/Cambridge MA: CABI Publishing.

Dorward, A. and J. Kydd, 2004: "The Malawi 2002 Food Crisis: The Rural Development Challenge", *Journal of Modern Africa Studies* 42(3):343-61.

Dorward, A., R.S. Wheeler, I. Mac Auslan, C.P. Buckley, J. Kydd and E. Chirwa, 2006: *Promoting Agriculture for Social Protection or Social Protection for Agriculture: Policy and Research Issues,* Future Agricultures, ODI, London.

Easterly, W. and R. Levine, 1997: "Africa's Growth Tragedy: Policies and Ethnic Division", *Quarterly Journal of Economics* 112(4):1203-50.

Ehrenpreis, D., 2009: "Poverty – What it is and what to do about it —Ideas and Policies in the International Community and in Swedish Development Cooperation" (mimeo).

Ekeland, 2009: "Havelmoo – a low key heterodox?" (mimeo).

Elbers, C., J-W. Gunning and L. Pan, 2009: "Growing out of Poverty under Risk: Evidence from Rural Ethiopia", Department of Economics, VU University, Amsterdam and Tinbergen Institute, Amsterdam.

Elbers, C., J-W. Gunning and B. Kinsey, 2007: "Growth and Risk: Methodology and Micro Evidence", *World Bank Economic Review* 21:1-20.

Foster, J., J. Greer and E. Thorbecke, 1984: "A Class of Decomposable Poverty Measures", *Econometrica* 52(3).

Fosu, A.K., 2009: "Inequality and the Impact of Growth on Poverty: Comparative Evidence for Sub-Saharan Africa", *Journal of Development Studies* 45(5):726-45.

Grimm, M. and I. Günther, 2004: "How to Acheive Pro-Poor Growth in a Poor Economy – The Case of Burkina Faso", paper for the Operationalising pro-Poor Growth project, AMB, BTZ, DFID and World Bank, Washington DC.

–, 2006: "Growth and Poverty in Burkina Faso: A Reassessment of the Paradox", in *Journal of African Economies* 15(3), March.

Guillaumont, P., S. Guillaumont and J.F. Brun, 1999: "How Instability Lowers African Growth", *Journal of African Economies* 8(17):87-107.

Hårsmar, M. 2004: "Heavy Clouds but No Rain – Agricultural Growth Theories and Peasant Strategies on the Mossi Plateau, Burkina Faso", Dissertation Agraria 439, Swedish University of Agricultural Sciences, Uppsala.

Hoffmann, V., P. Karfakis and L. Christiaenssen, 2007: "Assets, Livelihoods and Poverty", pp 11-27 in L. Christiaensen and A. Sarris (eds): *Rural household vulnerability and insurance against commodity risks – Evidence from the United Republic of Tanzania*. Rome: FAO, Trade and Markets Division.

Jerven, M., 2009: "The Quest for the African Dummy: Explaining African Post-colonial Economic Performance Revisited", *Journal of International Development*, Published online 30 June.

Kalwij, A. and A. Vershoor, 2007: "Not by Growth Alone: The Role of the Distribution of Income in Regional Diversity in Poverty Reduction", *European Economic Review* 51(4):805-29.

Kanbur, R. and P. Shaffer, 2005: "Epistemology, Normative Theory and Poverty Analysis: Implications for Q-Squared in Practice", Working Paper 2, Q-Squared, University of Toronto.

Kenny, C. and M. Syrquin, 1999: "Growth and Transformation in East Africa" (mimeo), paper presented at World Bank workshop in Dar es Salaam, Tanzania, 6-7 May.

Kenny, C. and D. Williams, 2001: "What Do We Know About Economic Growth? Or, Why Don't We Know Very Much?", *World Development* 29(1):1-22.

Krishna, A., 2007: "Escaping Poverty and Becoming Poor in Three States of India, with Additional Evidence from Kenya, Uganda and Peru", in Narayan, D. and P. Patesch (eds): *Moving Out of Poverty – Cross-Disciplinary Perspectives on Mobility*. London: Palgrave; Washington DC: World Bank.

Kristensson Uggla, B., 2002: "Slaget om verkligheten – filosofi, omvärldsanalys, tolkning", Symposion, Lund.

Lachaud, J-P. 2002: "La dynamique de pauvreté au Burkina Faso revisitée: pauvreté durable et transistoire, et vulnerabilité", Université Montesquieu-Bordeaux IV.

–, 2003: "Dynamique de pauvreté, inégalité et urbanization au Burkina Faso", Presses Universitaires de Bordeaux.

–, 2004: "La pauvreté a-t-elle diminué ou augmenté au Burkina Faso? Evidence empirique fondée sur une approche non monétaire micro-multidimensionelle", Document de travail 103, Centre d'économie du développement, IFREDE-GRES, Université-Bordeaux IV.

–, 2005: "A la recherché de l'insaisissable dynamique de pauvreté au Burkina Faso. Une nouvelle evidence empirique", Document de travail 117, Centre d'économie du développement, IFREDE-GRES, Université-Bordeaux IV.

Larsson, R., 2001: "Between crisis and opportunity – Livelihoods, diversification and inequality among the Meru of Tanzania", dissertation, Sociology department, Lund University.

Lesamana, A.M.J., 2009: "Transition from Subsistence to Monetary Economy – A Counter Discource to Mainstream Development Strategies", Master's Thesis, Development Management, University of Agder, Kristiansand.

McGregor, S., 2008: "Poverty Reduction Slow Despite Economic Growth", IPS, Dar Es Salaam.

Ministry of the Economy and Finance, 2007: "Progress Report on the Implementation of the PRSP for Year 2006", Ouagadougou, Burkina Faso.

Nussbaum, M.C., 2006: *Frontiers of Justice – Disability, Nationality, Species Membership*. Cambridge MA: Belknap/Harvard University Press.

Oksen, P., 2001: "Agricultural Expansion and Animal Husbandry in a West African Savannah Environment" in Benjaminsen, T. and C. Lund (eds): *Politics, Property and Production in the West African Sahel – Understanding Natural Resource Management*. Uppsala: The Nordic Africa Institute.

OPHI, 2007: "Annex: OPHI Research Agenda Details", Queen Elizabeth House, Oxford University

Ponte, S., 2002: *Farmers and Markets in Tanzania*. Oxford: James Currey; Dar es Salaam: Mkuki na Nyota; Portsmouth: Heinemann.

Ravallion, M. 2001: "Growth, Inequality and Poverty: Looking Beyond Averages", *World Development* 29(11):1803-15.

–, 2010: "Why Don't We See Poverty Convergence?" (mimeo), World Bank, Washington DC.

Ravallion, M., S. Chen and P. Sangraula, 2008: "Dollar a Day Revisited" (mimeo), World Bank, Washington DC.

Ruggeri Laderchi, C., R. Saith and F. Stewart, 2006: "Does the Definition of Poverty Matter? – Comparing four approaches" in *Poverty in Focus*, UNDP International Poverty Centre, December 2006.

Sarris, A. and P. Karfakis, 2006: "Household Vulnerability in Rural Tanzania", CSAE Conference, St Catherine's College, Oxford.

Sen, A., 1999: *Development as Freedom*. Oxford/ New York: Oxford University Press.

Shaffer, P., 1998: "Gender, Poverty and Deprivation: Evidence from the Republic of Guinea", *World Development* 26(12):2119-35.

Son, H. and N. Kakwani, 2006: "Global Estimates of Pro-Poor Growth", IPC Working Paper Series 31, IPC, Brazil.

Tesulic E. D., 2004: "Burkina Faso: Quid de la Pauvreté?" (mimeo), Institut national de la statistique et de la démographie, Ouagadougou.

Tilly, C., 2007: "Poverty and the Politics of Exclusion" in Narayan, D. and P. Patesch (eds): *Moving Out of Poverty – Cross-Disciplinary Perspectives on Mobility*. London: Palgrave; Wahsington DC: World Bank.

UN DESA, 2004: *World Urbanization Prospects, The 2003 revision, Data Tables and Highlights*. New York: Population Division.

US Census Bureau, International Data Base (www.census.gov/ipc/, accessed 2009/08/04).

von Wright, G.H., 1971: *Explanation and Understanding*. London: Routledge and Kegan Paul.

World Bank, 2007: *Africa Development Indicators*, Washington DC.

–, 2008: *Poverty Data – A Supplement to World Development Indicators 2008*, Washington DC.

CURRENT AFRICAN ISSUES PUBLISHED BY THE INSTITUTE
Recent issues in the series are available electronically
for download free of charge www.nai.uu.se

1. *South Africa, the West and the Frontline States. Report from a Seminar.*1981, 34 pp
2. Maja Naur, *Social and Organisational Change in Libya.* 1982, 33 pp
3. *Peasants and Agricultural Production in Africa. A Nordic Research Seminar. Follow-up Reports and Discussions.* 1981, 34 pp
4. Ray Bush & S. Kibble, *Destabilisation in Southern Africa, an Overview.* 1985, 48 pp
5. Bertil Egerö, *Mozambique and the Southern African Struggle for Liberation.* 1985, 29 pp
6. Carol B.Thompson, *Regional Economic Polic under Crisis Condition. Southern African Development.*1986, 34 pp
7. Inge Tvedten, *The War in Angola, Internal Conditions for Peace and Recovery.* 1989, 14 pp
8. Patrick Wilmot, *Nigeria's Southern Africa Policy 1960–1988.* 1989, 15 pp
9. Jonathan Baker, *Perestroika for Ethiopia: In Search of the End of the Rainbow?* 1990, 21 pp
10. Horace Campbell, *The Siege of Cuito Cuanavale.* 1990, 35 pp
11. Maria Bongartz, *The Civil War in Somalia. Its genesis and dynamics.* 1991, 26 pp
12. S.B.O. Gutto, *Human and People's Rights in Africa. Myths, Realities and Prospects.* 1991, 26 pp
13. Said Chikhi, Algeria. *From Mass Rebellion to Workers' Protest.* 1991, 23 pp
14. Bertil Odén, *Namibia's Economic Links to South Africa.* 1991, 43 pp
15. Cervenka Zdenek, *African National Congress Meets Eastern Europe. A Dialogue on Common Experience*s. 1992, 49 pp, ISBN 91-7106-337-4
16. Diallo Garba, Mauritania–The Other Apartheid? 1993, 75 pp, ISBN 91-7106-339-0
17. Zdenek Cervenka and Colin Legum, *Can National Dialogue Break the Power of Terror in Burundi?* 1994, 30 pp, ISBN 91-7106-353-6

18. Erik Nordberg and Uno Winblad, *Urban Environmental Health and Hygiene in Sub-Saharan Africa.* 1994, 26 pp, ISBN 91-7106-364-1
19. Chris Dunton and Mai Palmberg, *Human Rights and Homosexuality in Southern Africa.* 1996, 48 pp, ISBN 91-7106-402-8
20. Georges Nzongola-Ntalaja *From Zaire to the Democratic Republic of the Congo.* 1998, 18 pp, ISBN 91-7106-424-9
21. Filip Reyntjens, *Talking or Fighting? Political Evolution in Rwanda and Burundi, 1998–1999.* 1999, 27 pp, ISBN 91-7106-454-0
22. Herbert Weiss, *War and Peace in the Democratic Republic of the Congo.* 1999, 28 pp, ISBN 91-7106-458-3
23. Filip Reyntjens, *Small States in an Unstable Region – Rwanda and Burundi, 1999–2000,* 2000, 24 pp, ISBN 91-7106-463-X
24. Filip Reyntjens, *Again at the Crossroads: Rwanda and Burundi, 2000–2001.* 2001, 25 pp, ISBN 91-7106-483-4
25. Henning Melber, *The New African Initiative and the African Union. A Preliminary Assessment and Documentation.* 2001, 36 pp, ISBN 91-7106-486-9
26. Dahilon Yassin Mohamoda, *Nile Basin Cooperation. A Review of the Literature.* 2003, 39 pp, ISBN 91-7106-512-1
27. Henning Melber (ed.), *Media, Public Discourse and Political Contestation in Zimbabwe.* 2004, 39 pp, ISBN 91-7106-534-2
28. Georges Nzongola-Ntalaja, *From Zaire to the Democratic Republic of the Congo. Second and Revised Edition.* 2004, 23 pp, ISBN-91-7106-538-5
29. Henning Melber (ed.), *Trade, Development, Cooperation – What Future for Africa?* 2005, 44 pp, ISBN 91-7106-544-X
30. Kaniye S.A. Ebeku, *The Succession of Faure Gnassingbe to the Togolese Presidency – An International Law Perspective.* 2005, 32 pp, ISBN 91-7106-554-7

31. Jeffrey V. Lazarus, Catrine Christiansen, Lise Rosendal Østergaard, Lisa Ann Richey, *Models for Life – Advancing antiretroviral therapy in sub-Saharan Africa*.
2005, 33 pp, ISBN 91-7106-556-3

32. Charles Manga Fombad and Zein Kebonang, *AU, NEPAD and the APRM – Democratisation Efforts Explored. Edited by Henning Melber*.
2006, 56 pp, ISBN 91-7106-569-5

33. Pedro Pinto Leite, Claes Olsson, Magnus Schöldtz, Toby Shelley, Pål Wrange, Hans Corell and Karin Scheele, *The Western Sahara Conflict – The Role of Natural Resources in Decolonization. Edited by Claes Olsson*.
2006, 32 pp, ISBN 91-7106-571-7

34. Jassey, Katja and Stella Nyanzi, *How to Be a "Proper" Woman in the Times of HIV and AIDS*.
2007, 35 pp, ISBN 91-7106-574-1

35. Lee, Margaret, Henning Melber, Sanusha Naidu and Ian Taylor, *China in Africa. Compiled by Henning Melber*.
2007, 47 pp, ISBN 978-91-7106-589-6

36. Nathaniel King, *Conflict as Integration. Youth Aspiration to Personhood in the Teleology of Sierra Leone's 'Senseless War'*.
2007, 32 pp, ISBN 978-91-7106-604-6

37. Aderanti Adepoju, *Migration in sub-Saharan Africa*.
2008. 70 pp, ISBN 978-91-7106-620-6

38. Bo Malmberg, *Demography and the development potential of sub-Saharan Africa*.
2008, 39 pp, 978-91-7106-621-3

39. Johan Holmberg, *Natural resources in sub-Saharan Africa: Assets and vulnerabilities*.
2008, 52 pp, 978-91-7106-624-4

40. Arne Bigsten and Dick Durevall, *The African economy and its role in the world economy*.
2008, 66 pp, 978-91-7106-625-1

41. Fantu Cheru, *Africa's development in the 21st century: Reshaping the research agenda*.
2008, 47 pp, 978-91-7106-628-2

42. Dan Kuwali, *Persuasive Prevention. Towards a Principle for Implementing Article 4(h) and R2P by the African Union*.
2009. 70 pp. ISBN 978-91-7106-650-3

43. Daniel Volman, *China, India, Russia and the United States. The Scramble for African Oil and the Militarization of the Continent*.
2009. 24 pp. ISBN 978-91-7106-658-9

44. Mats Hårsmar, *Understanding Poverty in Africa? A Navigation through Disputed Concepts, Data and Terrains*.
2010. 54 pp. ISBN 978-91-7106-668-8

www.ingramcontent.com/pod-product-compliance
Lightning Source LLC
Chambersburg PA
CBHW080056280326
41934CB00014B/3337